FLEXIBLE BENEFI

Motivation and Cost Con

FLEXIBLE BENEFITS

MOTIVATION AND COST CONTROL

Coopers
&Lybrand

CCH Editions Limited
TAX, BUSINESS AND LAW PUBLISHERS

Published by CCH Editions Limited
Telford Road, Bicester, Oxfordshire OX6 0XD
Tel. (0869) 253300, Facsimile (0869) 245814.
DX: 83750 Bicester 2

USA	Commerce Clearing House, Inc., Chicago, Illinois.
CANADA	CCH Canadian Limited, Toronto, Ontario.
AUSTRALIA	CCH Australia Limited, North Ryde, NSW.
NEW ZEALAND	CCH New Zealand Limited, Auckland.
SINGAPORE	CCH Asia Limited.
JAPAN	CCH Japan Limited.

This publication is designed to provide accurate and authoritative information in regard to the subject-matter covered. It is sold with the understanding that the publisher is not engaged in rendering legal or other professional services. If legal advice or other expert assistance is required, the services of a competent professional person should be sought.

Ownership of Trade Marks

The Trade Marks

CCH ACCESS, COMPUTAX and **COMMERCE CLEARING HOUSE, INC.**
are the property of Commerce Clearing House, Incorporated, Chicago, Illinois, USA

British Library Cataloguing-in-Publication Data.

Coopers & Lybrand
  Flexible Benefits: Motivation and Cost
  Control
  I. Title
  331.2550941

ISBN 0 86325 318 0

© 1993 Coopers & Lybrand

All rights reserved. No part of this work may be reproduced or copied in any form or by any means (graphic, electronic or mechanical, including photocopying, recording, recording taping, or information and retrieval systems) without the written permission of the copyright holders.

Typeset in Great Britain by Mendip Communications Ltd, Frome, Somerset.
Printed and bound in Great Britain by The Eastern Press Limited, Reading, Berkshire.

Preface

During the 1980s, flexible benefits packages looked set to take off in the UK. Demographic indicators were showing a probable shortfall in available personnel for the future, and staff in many professions were still highly mobile between organisations. Employers were looking for creative ways to attract and retain their workforces. Flexible benefits packages it seemed could offer staff a choice of benefits to suit their lifestyle needs. This aspect was particularly important for employers who were, for example, trying to attract women back to work, or to satisfy the needs of staff in dual income families.

Flexible benefits packages, or 'flex', had become a typical component of the reward package in the US. The incentive to introduce such plans was very different from the issues in the UK. Escalating medical insurance costs in a country where employers are obliged to provide such cover required companies to find a way in which to contain costs. Flex provided the opportunity to pass on benefit cost increases to the employee, and to strengthen management control over benefits usage so that the employer was getting value for money on its benefits spend.

By the end of the 1980s, recession had taken hold in the UK. Far from seeking to attract and retain staff, employers were fighting to keep their businesses viable, and, in many cases, were laying staff off, or, at minimum, imposing headcount freezes. Few organisations saw the need to divert attention to benefits arrangements. In any case, during this period many staff were employed on part-time, or flexible hours contracts, which do not attract the same range of benefits as those for full-time staff.

Although lessons from the US showed that flexible benefits offered opportunities for cost control, or cost reduction, the amounts which could be saved were trivial compared with the net gain of stripping out non-productive business units, or downsizing activities. Furthermore, the employee or industrial relations implications of introducing flex for remaining employees in an atmosphere of uncertainty and insecurity deterred some organisations which might otherwise have made the change for financial reasons.

As we emerge from recession it appears that flex is back on the agenda. The labour market is becoming more mobile again, and retention is increasingly a critical personnel management issue. There has been considerable interest in flex in professional publications for human resources managers and benefits advisers and, between press coverage on the one hand, and fully implemented plans on the other, increasing numbers of companies have flex on their agenda, or at the more active end of their wish lists. However, as yet there are few company-wide flex plans in the UK. Often those companies which have made the change are international companies, or UK subsidiaries of US parents, which have cascaded plans designed in other country operations (with the benefit of their experience). A few UK organisations have introduced schemes which are limited to discrete, and most frequently, senior groups of personnel.

It is not surprising, therefore, that, beyond press articles, most of the literature about flexible benefits is from US publications about US plans. If your company is considering changing your benefits regime to one of flexible choice, you are likely to find a bewildering array of plans in the existing sources, many of them probably unsuitable for the UK market.

This book provides a readable and practical guide for organisations considering the introduction of flexible benefits packages and Chapter 2 contains a question and answer section tackling the fundamental questions. At first sight, the change may seem to be a costing and analytical exercise to be carried out by the benefits adviser. Indeed, the costing and pricing issues are complex areas, and the book looks at how to design your plan and to set the financial parameters. However, this type of analysis is only one aspect of the change to benefits arrangements. The book provides guidance on other areas, including how to ensure the new benefits arrangements support organisational objectives; the tax and legal implications of the changes; administration of the plan and how to manage the consultation and communication process. It also considers how to apply flexible benefits in the international context.

This book is an essential guide to coping with the change to flexible benefits, and the wider organisational issues which have to be taken into consideration to ensure that the new arrangements are accepted and endorsed by the workforce. The issues in design and implementation are illustrated with case studies from organisations which have plans operating successfully both in the US and the UK.

This book is essentially about 'how to' introduce a flexible benefits plan, and to flag some of the organisational, actuarial, tax and legal issues. While we are confident that it will enable readers to understand how to set up a plan, we must advise them to confirm their arrangements with the Inland Revenue and their professional advisers, particularly in the area of long-term risk benefits, such as pensions, before taking action.

Coopers & Lybrand
September 1993

About the Publisher

CCH Editions Limited is part of a world-wide group of companies that specialises in tax, business and law publishing. The group produces a wide range of books and reporting services for the accounting, business and legal professions. The Oxfordshire premises are the centre for all UK and European operations.

All CCH publications are designed to be practical and authoritative and are written by CCH's own highly qualified and experienced editorial team and specialist outside authors.

In the UK CCH Editions currently produces a comprehensive series of reporting services on UK and international tax, business and law, and many books covering specific areas of interest for accountants, lawyers and business managers. Irrespective of the subject matter being discussed or the depth and scope of its treatment, the material is always dealt with in the same clear and concise manner.

CCH is committed to you and your information needs, and this commitment is reflected in the constant updating and development of our reporting services and the growth and expansion of our range of publications.

If you would like to know more about our books or loose-leaf services telephone (0869) 253300.

About the Author

Coopers & Lybrand is one of the United Kingdom's leading firms of chartered accountants and business advisers. To write this book, the firm has drawn on contributions from experts in a wide range of professional disciplines. We recognise that no single practitioner can provide the depth of expertise required in each of the professional disciplines to design and implement a successful flexible benefits plan. Principal contributors are as follows:

- The editors, Moira Conoley and Gill Sivyer are key members of the Coopers & Lybrand Reward Practice, which includes pay, actuarial, tax, legal and human resource management specialists.
- Technical contributions to the book were also written by Carol Woodley, Neville Mackay and Sandeep Varma, who are all qualified actuaries; Clive Tulloch and Judy Brown, tax specialists; and Tim Johnson, an employment law practitioner.

Coopers & Lybrand is authorised by the Institute of Chartered Accountants in England and Wales to carry on investment business.

Acknowledgements

We are grateful to those authors and organisations who have kindly provided case study experiences to illustrate the different issues which may arise in implementing flexible benefits arrangements:

- Dick Quinn, Director, Corporate Benefit Planning and Services Manager, PSE&G
- Laura Colella, Director of Employee Benefits, Saatchi & Saatchi North America Inc.
- Gail DeGroat, Director of Benefits and Personnel Administration, D'Arcy Masius Benton & Bowles, Inc.
- Marilyn Gay, Director of Benefits, Keycorp Bank
- Keith Wilkinson, Human Resources Manager, CIGNA Insurance Services
- Laurence Moss, Human Resources Manager, Colgate Palmolive.

We would also like to thank professional advisers who have provided details of their administration systems (Appendix 3):

- Hewitt Associates
- Noble Lowndes
- Towers Perrin
- William M. Mercer Limited
- The Wyatt Company.

Contents

	Page
Preface	v
About the Publisher	vii
About the Author	viii
Acknowledgements	ix
Glossary	xvii

1 Introduction — 1
- ¶101 What is a flexible benefits approach? — 1
- ¶102 Implementing flexible benefits is not just about designing a new plan — 1
- ¶103 The need for a project team — 2
- ¶104 Introducing flexible benefits is a major project — 3
- ¶105 Moving to phase two – the design loop — 4
- ¶106 So, you still want to proceed? — 5

2 Key Issues: Questions and Answers on Flexible Benefits — 6
- ¶201 Introduction — 6
- ¶202 What can I get out of this book? — 6
- ¶203 What are 'flexible benefits'? — 6
- ¶204 What are core benefits? — 6
- ¶205 What is wrong with just cash? — 7
- ¶206 Do moves to neutralise the tax advantages of benefits make flex less attractive? — 7
- ¶207 Why should I be considering flexible benefits? — 7
- ¶208 Why should the workforce be interested in flexible benefits? — 7
- ¶209 How many organisations already run such plans? — 7
- ¶210 Can we import a plan from the US? — 8
- ¶211 Do flexible benefits plans work throughout Europe? — 8
- ¶212 Are flexible benefits suitable for any size of organisation, in any sector? — 8
- ¶213 Can I save money by introducing flexible benefits? — 8
- ¶214 How much will flexible benefits cost? — 8
- ¶215 How long will it take to introduce a flexible benefits plan? — 9

Contents   xi

		Page
¶216	Which benefits are usually included in a flexible benefits plan?	9
¶217	Which benefits are typically avoided?	9
¶218	If I have flexed one or two benefits, what are the next steps?	10
¶219	Should I include pensions?	10
¶220	Which benefits are tax-free?	11
¶221	Which benefits are tax efficient?	12
¶222	Will flexible benefits change the tax efficiency of the benefits I already offer?	12
¶223	How do I price the benefits?	12
¶224	What would stop me introducing a flexible benefits plan?	13
¶225	Will my employees understand flexible benefits?	13
¶226	Can I make the proposed flexible benefits plan compulsory?	13
¶227	Can I introduce flexible benefits into a unionised company?	14
¶228	What do I do if my employees do not want to join the flexible benefits plan?	14
¶229	Do I need to change my existing employment contracts?	14
¶230	How do I administer a flexible benefits plan?	15
¶231	What can go wrong?	15
¶232	Do I need professional advice?	15

3 Flexible Benefits are About Choice   16

	Executive summary	16
¶301	Introduction	17
¶302	Choice (*chois*) n	17
¶303	Why do employers want to offer more choice?	17
¶304	Why do employees want more choice?	19
¶305	The scope for choice	19
¶306	Choice between benefits	19
¶307	Choice in paying for benefits	20
¶308	Why not flexible benefits?	21
¶309	If choice is so wonderful, why are there so few plans in operation in the UK?	21
¶310	The benefit of choice	22
¶311	Flex: an example	22

4 Why Flexible Benefits? – Setting Objectives   26

	Executive summary	26
¶401	Motives for flexible benefits	26
¶402	Stated objectives	27
¶403	Some example objectives	27
¶404	The need for objectives	28

		Page
¶405	An opportunity to reconsider objectives	29
¶406	The need to revisit objectives	29

5 Costing the Current Benefits Package — 32

	Executive summary	32
¶501	Establish a cost baseline	32
¶502	Understanding the current cost	32
¶503	What to include	33
¶504	Analysing the data	33

6 Designing the Plan – The Key Parameters — 35

	Executive summary	35
¶601	The importance of objectives – revisited	35
¶602	Design parameters	35
¶603	Eligibility	36
¶604	Scope for choice	37
¶605	Benefits to be included	37
¶606	Timing of elections	38
¶607	Currency of pricing or credits	39
¶608	Plan design – some examples	39

7 Designing the Plan – The Major Benefits — 43

	Executive summary	43
¶701	Introduction	43
¶702	Company car	44
¶703	Pension	46
¶704	Life assurance	48
¶705	Medical insurance	49
¶706	Long-term disability insurance	51
¶707	Including holiday entitlement in flex plans	52
¶708	Other benefits	52

8 Pricing The New Benefits Package – Issues — 55

	Executive summary	55
¶801	Pricing an unknown quantity	55
¶802	Pricing philosophy – an overview	56
¶803	Pricing principles	57
¶804	Pricing philosophy – a dilemma	57
¶805	Pricing philosophy – a pragmatic approach	58
¶806	Setting the prices	58

		Page
¶807	The effects of selection	59
¶808	Company car	59
¶809	Risk benefits	60
¶810	Holiday entitlement	60
¶811	Other benefits	60

9 Setting Credit Allowances 63

	Executive summary	63
¶901	Introduction	63
¶902	What are credits?	63
¶903	How are the credits set?	63
¶904	Winners and losers	64
¶905	Two methods to drive credit allocations	64
¶906	A formula-driven approach	65
¶907	A tabular approach	67
¶908	Summing up	68

10 Costing the Plan 69

	Executive summary	69
¶1001	Introduction	69
¶1002	Developing a cost model	69
¶1003	Winners and losers	71
¶1004	Testing for robustness	72
¶1005	Closing the loop	73

11 Income Tax, National Insurance Contributions and VAT – in Relation to Flex 74

	Executive summary	74
¶1101	Taking taxes into account	74
¶1102	Income tax	75
¶1103	VAT	75
¶1104	National Insurance contributions	76
¶1105	Conclusion	76

12 Employment Law and Flexible Benefits 77

	Executive summary	77
¶1201	A change in employment contracts	77
¶1202	The need for employees' consent	78
¶1203	What if employees do not want flexible benefits?	78
¶1204	Equal pay and sex discrimination	78

		Page
¶1205	Summary checklist	79
¶1206	Drafting the plan	80
¶1207	Introducing the plan	81

13 Flexible Benefits for International Managers and Overseas Assignments 82

	Executive summary	82
¶1301	Cost control issues	82
¶1302	Motivational issues	83
¶1303	The current situation	83
¶1304	How flex might be introduced	83

14 Administration 84

	Executive summary	84
¶1401	Introduction	84
¶1402	The nature of the system	85
¶1403	Choosing a solution – the options	85
¶1404	Selecting a system – key functions	86
¶1405	Selecting a system – linking in	88
¶1406	Preparation and procedures	89
¶1407	Third-party administration	89
¶1408	Conclusion	89

15 Telling Staff about the Flexible Benefits Plan 94

	Executive summary	94
¶1501	The external context	94
¶1502	Communication is a project in its own right	94
¶1503	Set up a communications project team	95
¶1504	Testing the water	95
¶1505	The need for senior executive sponsorship	96
¶1506	Researching employees' opinions	96
¶1507	A two-way communication process	96
¶1508	Tell employees whether the project will proceed	97
¶1509	Consult employees at every stage in the project	97
¶1510	Pilot the communications media	98
¶1511	Plan the communications administration	98
¶1512	Communication is a phased process	99
¶1513	Key messages	99
¶1514	Match the media to the message	100
¶1515	Partners are part of the decision-making process	103
¶1516	Monitor the plan	103

		Page
¶1517	Summary	103

16 Implementation of Flexible Compensation at CIGNA Employee Benefits — 107

	Summary	107
¶1601	About CIGNA	107
¶1602	Preparation for flex – employee survey	107
¶1603	The external consultant	108
¶1604	Plan design	108
¶1605	Implementation	112
¶1606	Communication	112
¶1607	Understanding the choices made	113
¶1608	Helplines	114
¶1609	Benefit shifts	114
¶1610	Employer advantages	115
¶1611	Employee advantages	115
¶1612	Overview	115
¶1613	The future for flex – a comment from the editors	116

Appendix 1: Cash or Cars — 117

Avoiding the tax traps	117
Frequency of choice	117
The importance of contractual arrangements	117
Setting the cash alternative	118
Which motoring costs to compare	118
Taking account of National Insurance contributions	118
Cost of administration	118
Dealing with business mileage	118
Treatment of the cash allowance	119
Frequency of payment of the cash allowance	119

Appendix 2: The Tax Treatment of Flexible Compensation — 120

Introduction	120
Income tax	120
Value added tax	127
National Insurance contributions	129
Flexible compensation and notional salaries	130
The legal relationship	131

Appendix 3: Flexible Benefits Administration Systems — 132

Coopers & Lybrand	132

xvi   *Flexible Benefits*

	Page
Hewitt Associates	133
Noble Lowndes	135
Towers Perrin	137
William M. Mercer Limited	138
The Wyatt Company	139
Index	141

Glossary

Algorithm: a formula or rule for calculating an assigned quantity often by an iterative process converging on the true value.

Contribution holiday: a period during which employers' and/or members' contributions to pension funds are temporarily suspended, normally when the fund is in surplus. The term is sometimes used loosely when contributions continue to be paid but at a reduced rate.

Cross-subsidies: these result when the combined benefit costs for groups of employees do not equate to the individual subgroups on their own. The situation arises that one subgroup is paying more and another less than it would be had it existed on its own.

Earnings cap: limitation introduced by the Finance Act 1989 on the amount of remuneration on which pension benefits and contributions, can be based. Broadly, it applies to members of schemes established on or after 14 March 1989 and all new members of schemes joining on or after 1 June 1989. For the tax years 1993/94, the cap stands at £75,000.

Equalising benefits: the costs arise from the requirement to treat either sex, in terms of benefits, no less favourably to the other. This arose from Article 119 of the Treaty of Rome and the subsequent European Court judgment in the *Barber* v *Guardian Royal Exchange Insurance* case.

Indemnity plans: indemnity plan is a health care plan that reimburses providers or covered participants for expenses incurred for medical treatment.

Regression techniques: statistical method aiming to find the parameters of a pre-defined function that best fit a set of data points.

Reimbursement accounts: reimbursement accounts are accounts funded by employer contributions, employee salary reductions, or both and the proceeds are applied to paying certain expenses incurred during the year.

Risk benefits: benefits arising from an event which is normally insurable. These include lump sums payable on death and income benefits payable on disability.

401(K): A US term for Code Sec. 401(K) Plans, referred to as cash or deferred arrangements (CODAs), allow an employee to choose whether the employer should pay a certain amount directly to the employee in cash, or instead pay that amount to a qualified plan on the employee's behalf.

1 Introduction

¶101 What is a flexible benefits approach?

In the UK, fringe benefits are increasingly becoming a significant proportion of employees' reward packages. The total cost of providing the same benefits to every employee or hierarchical level of employee is a major one. Yet current reward packages often fail to meet employees' needs at particular stages in their lives. Employees therefore seldom realise how much their benefits actually cost, and attach little importance to those benefits they do not use or value. For example, staff in their twenties rarely consider pension schemes to be worthwhile.

Flexible benefits plans offer employees choice. They can choose from a range of benefits although the choice available to them is sometimes limited by the employer through a menu approach, or by stipulating some mandatory benefits which the employee must take.

Flexible benefits allow employers to recognise the differing needs of their staff, permitting them to choose those benefits which are appropriate, and to determine the amount of money, if any, they wish to spend on further benefits.

From the employer's point of view, a flexible benefits plan provides scope to limit cost. The employer can decide how much the organisation will pay for its benefits plan, and limit benefits within the cost ceiling, or pass on increases in benefit prices to the employees.

¶102 Implementing flexible benefits is not just about designing a new plan

We are frequently asked about the design parameters for flexible benefits plans. However, the single most important message we offer is to recognise how far-reaching are the implications of introducing new arrangements.

To introduce a flexible benefits plan represents a fundamental change which can signal to employees a shift in the organisation's objectives and culture. It is, therefore, important to involve and consult employees from the initial stages, and to focus considerable effort on the communication of the new arrangements.

Changes to risk benefits, such as insurance and pensions, need to be carefully costed. Whilst most in-house departments can cope with costing a scheme which all employees join, the sensitivity analysis and actuarial projection required to cost a plan which depends on take-up is not a task to be undertaken lightly.

The changes in the benefits package will need to be reflected in the employees' employment contracts. It is essential to ensure that the employer's legal position is defensible, and to make arrangements for employees who choose not to join the plan, if that is to be allowed.

Tax legislation in respect of benefits is changing rapidly. Employers must ensure they understand the tax and National Insurance contribution liabilities that they, and their employees, will incur before the plan is implemented. Liaison with, and agreement from, the Inland Revenue and Customs and Excise is critical.

Many existing benefits arrangements require only minimal administration support, for example to record whether or not an employee is entitled to a particular benefit. Some benefits such as pensions or shares require more complex support, but are often administered on a benefit-by-benefit basis. A more flexible and sophisticated system will be required to support flexible benefits packages, one which will support all the benefits on offer, and which will record eligibility, elections and take-up, and do so without a significant increase in administrative workload.

¶103 The need for a project team

A project team is essential to pull together the multiple elements of such a major project. It requires strong project management, and the allocation of adequate resource to each activity.

It is vital that a project team is identified, and that they work to a structured project plan. Flexible benefits plans cannot be introduced effectively by treating the activities as part of the day-to-day work of the human resources department. There is a considerable resource requirement, and those involved must have time allocated for their tasks, defined objectives, and dates for completion.

The project team should include representatives from:

- senior staff who will make decisions about the new plan;
- staff responsible for the introduction of the plan, typically from the human resources function;
- staff responsible for administering current benefits, including pensions managers, finance staff who typically administer share schemes, car fleet managers, and payroll staff;

Introduction 3

- staff who will administer the new plan;
- representatives of those who will receive the new package;
- external agencies such as insurers, legal, pensions and tax advisers;
- staff from the information technology function who will be responsible for developing and/or running new systems.

Organisations with collective agreements should also consider union consultation or even involvement in the project team, depending on their style of consultation and negotiation.

In addition to this key project team, there will also need to be a communications project team, working at an operational level on the participation, involvement and implementation (see Chapter 15). There should be some common membership between the two teams, particularly from the human resources department, if it is to be responsible for the administration post introduction.

¶104 Introducing flexible benefits is a major project

Figure 1 sets out the major phases in a project to introduce flexible benefits:
- feasibility,
- design,
- implementation.

Phases:

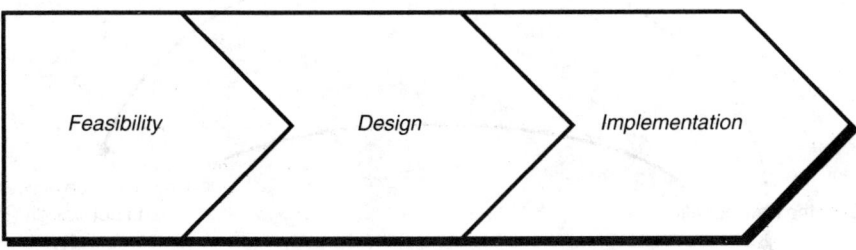

Stages:

- Set up a project team
- Objective setting
- Package review
- Administration review
- Contractual review
- Current benefits costing
- Employee research
- Feasibility assessment

- Set design criteria
- Design plan structure
- Benefit pricing
- 'Credits' policy
- Insurer liaison/self-insurance
- Revenue and Customs liaison
- Employment contracts
- Administration design
- Finalise design

- Communication
- Documentation
- Administration

Figure 1: Introducing flexible benefits

¶104

Few organisations recognise the number of activities or volume of work required in the feasibility phase. Many want to start at phase two, designing the plan.

Perhaps the most important element of phase one is at the end of it, the feasibility assessment. Each organisation must make a clear decision, based on considerable analysis of factual data and employee views, as to whether it will proceed ... or not.

¶105 Moving to phase two – the design loop

Two of the stages in phase one – objective setting and current benefits costing – provide a baseline for the design of the plan itself. The objectives and design parameters, such as who will be covered by the plan, and which benefits to include, will influence the benefit pricing stage, and in turn the cost of the benefits to the employer.

Typically the cost outcome at the first iteration is unlikely to fulfil the cost objectives the employer may have set itself, or the impact on affected staff may be unacceptable. It is often necessary to revisit the objectives and design parameters and to go round the pricing and costing loop again ... and possibly again.

The design loop is set out in Figure 2. It is worth noting that the model overall

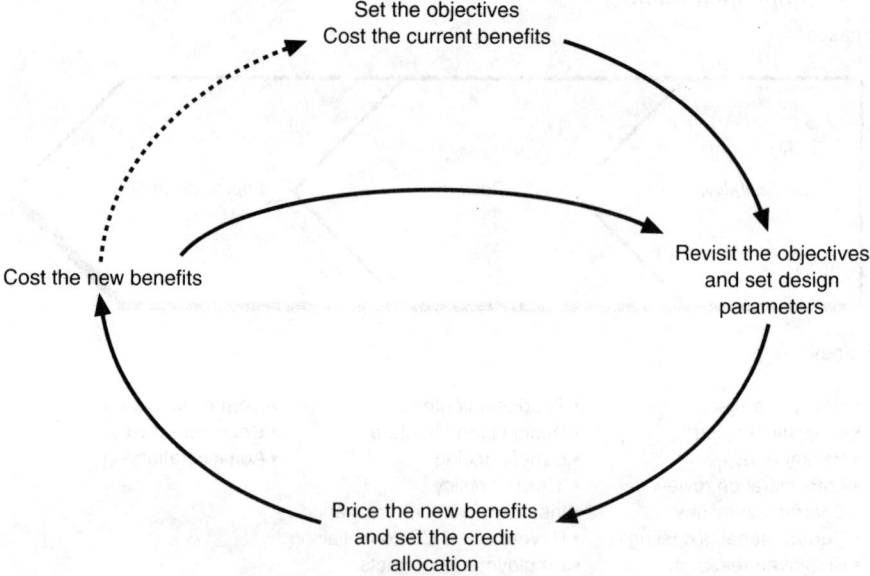

Figure 2: Flexible benefits – the design loop

should be revisited after implementation of the plan to ensure that the new benefits plan continues to match the organisation's reward objectives.

¶106 So, you still want to proceed?

The purpose of this book is to provide a readable and practical guide to the introduction of flexible benefits plans. We illustrate the issues with experiences from organisations which have hit some of the pitfalls, and overcome some of the obstacles. We also provide a number of checklists and proformas to guide you through the issues. However, there is no substitute for full and effective project management, and the involvement of the relevant technical experts and affected employees.

Note: it is in the nature of the subject discussed here that a number of technical terms, abbreviations and acronyms are used. If these are not explained where they first appear they are listed in a Glossary on p. xvii.

2 Key Issues: Questions and Answers on Flexible Benefits

¶201 Introduction

There are still very few flexible benefits plans in the UK which cover large numbers of employees, or a full range of benefits. Consequently, human resources managers considering introducing flexible benefits cannot yet draw on the experience of colleagues and peers in the UK. This chapter seeks to answer some questions asked by managers caught in the dilemma of drawing on US experience, which may be inappropriate, or going it alone.

¶202 What can I get out of this book?

Flexible benefits plans will be part of the remuneration policies of the 1990s. Forward-looking organisations will want to understand and evaluate flexibility options in order to choose the right route forward for them. Such organisations also recognise that flexible plans are complex to design and administer. This book highlights some of the practical and technical issues, and offers guidance on how to address them. Case studies from organisations which have implemented plans illustrate how they have tackled some of the pitfalls and obstacles. A number of checklists and *aides-mémoires* will help you to implement a successful project. The book on its own, however, is no substitute for advice from your professional advisers.

¶203 What are 'flexible benefits'?

Flexible benefits are a means by which employers offer their staff a choice of benefits, both between different benefits, and the level of each benefit. Each benefit has a price and each employee a pre-set spending limit. Employees choose those benefits which are most appropriate for them and their lifestyle.

¶204 What are core benefits?

In some flexible benefits plans, certain benefits are mandatory or core for all employees included in the plan. Each employee can then select from a further range of benefits to add to their core benefits.

Some employers provide core benefits which will ensure staff have a certain amount of security in terms of insurance and pensions. The core benefits offered will, of course, depend on the organisation's philosophy and culture.

¶205 What is wrong with just cash?

Cash is expensive. There are no group discounts for cash, as there are for many benefits. It also attracts tax and National Insurance contributions. When the labour market is buoyant, employees can change jobs at little or no cost if they receive no benefits. Other benefits, such as pensions, however, can increase retention.

¶206 Do moves to neutralise the tax advantages of benefits make flex less attractive?

No, the Government's moves to tax-neutralise benefits as compared with cash do not eliminate the other advantages that benefits can have over cash. In fact, a more level playing field between benefits and cash means that flexibility is more important, since standard benefits are no longer an obvious choice for all staff.

¶207 Why should I be considering flexible benefits?

Flexible benefits plans allow employers greater scope for cost control, and, if necessary, the chance to pass on increasing benefit costs to employees. The plan can make staff aware of the value of their benefits, yet at the same time provide greater motivation, since staff can choose the benefits which best suit them.

¶208 Why should the workforce be interested in flexible benefits?

Today's workforce is no longer made up from conventional socio-economic stereotypes. For example, dual-income families, single parents, and women returning to work all have special needs, as do those at different stages in their life and career. Flexible benefits give staff the opportunity to choose the benefits which suit their particular circumstances and, if the scheme design allows, to decide how much of their own income they wish to spend on additional benefits.

¶209 How many organisations already run such plans?

Only a handful of large organisations in the UK have full-blown flexible benefits plans, but most organisations have flexible plans in one form or another, be it offering a choice between a company car or cash, or an element of choice at the recruitment stage. There is a danger that, if an organisation does not address flexibility in a coherent manner, it will end up with a series of cash or benefit plans, with long-serving employees resentful of the better packages of new recruits.

¶210 Can we import a plan from the US?

The US plan is probably an American tax favoured 'cafeteria plan' which offers primarily insurance benefits which are either not tax favoured in the UK, or are only tax favoured in the UK as part of a tax-favoured pension scheme. A proper analysis of UK circumstances is essential.

¶211 Do flexible benefits plans work throughout Europe?

Yes. The position in each country needs to be looked at separately, but the basic attractions of flexible benefits apply across Europe. They can also help at the international expatriate level, by facilitating the tailoring of benefit plans to suit individual nationalities.

¶212 Are flexible benefits suitable for any size of organisation, in any sector?

Yes. Flexible benefits can work well in a wide range of organisations depending more on culture than size, or industry. Naturally, UK companies with American parents will often find that the concept is readily accepted by both management and staff.

¶213 Can I save money by introducing flexible benefits?

You are unlikely to make immediate cost savings as the opportunities for greater cost control usually take some time to come through. This is because the main financial advantage to companies is that future increases in benefit costs can be shared with employees as flexible benefits can provide the control mechanisms to do this.

If an organisation needs to cap or eliminate a particular benefit and is prepared to accept the consequences of doing this in terms of employee relations, the pill can be sweetened through introducing more choice at the same time. In this way flex can help to facilitate immediate savings, but care needs to be taken because the plan may become tainted with the unpleasant taste of the cut-back.

¶214 How much will flexible benefits cost?

There are a number of possible costs:
- administration systems,
- additional manpower to run the plan or third party costs,
- consultancy fees,

- additional costs from equalising benefits through the plan.

These will always need to be determined at an early stage – ideally before deciding to go ahead. All of these items depend on the complexity and coverage of the plan and could range from, say, £10,000 to £100,000.

¶215 How long will it take to introduce a flexible benefits plan?

Many organisations considering flexible benefits recognise the complexity of pricing existing and proposed benefits, and designing a plan, and allow sufficient time for these activities. However, few organisations make adequate plans for consulting with staff at the feasibility and design testing stages. In particular, the time and effort it takes to communicate the details of the plan, together with the time required for decision making are frequently overlooked. Even senior staff are likely to need considerable support and advice when making their initial elections.

From the early consideration of a plan to employees making their first election could take around nine months. Even longer may be needed if several plans are introduced, or the approach is introduced in more than one location.

¶216 Which benefits are usually included in a flexible benefits plan?

The company car will often be top of the list for company and employee alike. Other benefits which are often included are:

- medical expenses cover,
- life assurance,
- long-term disability insurance,
- money-purchase pension,
- child care vouchers,
- dental and/or eyecare insurance,
- counselling.

¶217 Which benefits are typically avoided?

Benefits which are difficult (but not impossible) to include are final salary pension schemes, mortgages and loans. These are usually excluded because of difficulties in pricing these benefits in a manner which is both safe (for the company) and meaningful. However, there are merits in including those benefits, so do not dismiss them.

¶217

¶218 If I have flexed one or two benefits, what are the next steps?

Sensible next steps may be:

- to review experience with existing benefits:
    - employee attitudes: eligible and non-eligible,
    - administration,
    - cost,
    - performance of plan against objectives;
- to decide on future company objectives and, if a change is to be made, the desired scope of the plan:
    - eligibility,
    - benefits,
    - extent of options;
- to price the benefit options and develop the detail of plan;
- to plan and execute implementation:
    - communication,
    - documentation,
    - administration.

¶219 Should I include pensions?

Pensions pose a tricky question. This is often one of the most significant benefits and one which typically suffers from a lack of employee appreciation. Employer costs are high and the cost control advantages of flexible benefits would also be valuable in many cases.

However, there are some technical issues. Firstly, any company with a contribution holiday will know about the cash flow advantages – these will be lost if any sort of cash alternative is offered. Secondly, the cost of 'final salary' pensions increases dramatically with age and this may need to be reflected in the pricing of options. This might be seen as unfairly penalising older staff and, given the significance of the pension benefit, be judged to be unacceptable. On the other hand, flat-rate option prices can open both the pension and flex plans to the risk of increased costs from 'anti-selection' because those for whom pensions are expensive will choose pensions whilst the rest will choose cash or other benefits. The overall effect is to raise costs. An example of how a pension scheme was successfully incorporated into a benefits plan is given in Case Study 1.

Case Study 1
As a result of several acquisitions a company was operating a number of final salary pension schemes. Along with the introduction of a flexible benefits plan, the company was keen to rationalise its pension arrangements. It recognised the difficulties in incorporating a final salary pension scheme within a flexible benefits plan but there was considerable resistance from the workforce to a change from final salary to money purchase pension provision.

The company successfully incorporated pensions within the flexible benefits plan by offering a core final salary pension benefit at a relatively modest level with pensions being based upon an accrual rate of 1/80th. Employees could opt for higher levels of pension provision but the excess benefits were provided on a money purchase basis. The company was therefore able to achieve its main aims, being:

- to rationalise its pension arrangements;
- to provide a core final salary pension benefit;
- to provide excess pension benefits under a money purchase basis, thereby simplifying the costing process.

¶220 Which benefits are tax-free?

Subject to certain conditions:

- car parking;
- pension contributions;
- life assurance, death in service, permanent disability insurance;
- luncheon vouchers up to 15p per day (any excess is not subject to NIC, but is subject to PAYE);
- free non-alcoholic refreshments (tea, coffee, etc.);
- meals taken whilst working 'out of hours';
- holidays;
- interest on loans where the interest is less than £300 per annum;
- accommodation where employees are required to live on employer's premises;
- outplacement counselling;
- professional advice provided in-house where no external costs are incurred;
- sports facilities provided by the employer;
- canteens provided they are available to all employees;
- first-aid allowances;

¶220

- long service gifts provided that the gift is not cash;
- medical insurance where travelling on business, and subsequent treatment, provided it is overseas;
- medical examinations;
- credit card subscriptions and membership fees;
- spouse's travel if it is required for his/her partner's job;
- uniforms;
- staff entertaining – maximum £50 per staff member and family;
- child care arrangements where the employer is partly or wholly responsible for finance and management of the facilities.

¶221 Which benefits are tax efficient?

The following may be tax efficient if the taxable benefit is less than the cost that the employee would have to outlay if they were providing the services or goods for themselves:

- accommodation;
- cars;
- personal use of a business asset;
- loan interest, depending on the interest rate charged by the employer.

¶222 Will flexible benefits change the tax efficiency of the benefits I already offer?

The introduction of a plan will necessitate the review of existing benefits, the integration of those benefits into the new plan and new agreement by the Inland Revenue to the tax treatment of the plan. Agreements from the past may be set aside.

¶223 How do I price the benefits?

This is a very complex area to which a whole book could be devoted. Briefly, the starting point is the current cost of each benefit. This needs to be analysed and a clear picture built up of the factors underlying this cost for example, the individual ages, salary, sex, etc. and, perhaps, the experience of a group covered by an insured arrangement. Research needs to be done into the likely effects of offering employees options on these costs so that the pricing system can be based on realistic longer term estimates.

Decisions need to be taken on the pricing philosophy. For example, you may want to make sure that employees know the true cost of providing each benefit to them individually, but you may also feel uncomfortable about prices increasing with age. Objectives need to be prioritised and these conflicts resolved in order to arrive at a clear set of principles. These will then allow a full pricing system to be developed from the data on current and future benefit costs.

¶224 What would stop me introducing a flexible benefits plan?

In some circumstances, an employer may need to impose flexible benefits or other contractual changes on staff for business reasons, particularly if the changes are driven by cost constraints. However, if the reason for change is to best meet the differing needs of staff, it is important to listen to their views, and only to introduce the change if the employees want it.

¶225 Will my employees understand flexible benefits?

Our experience shows that even senior employees do not fully understand their benefits arrangements. Flexible benefits plans are typically more complex than conventional plans, and it is critical that employees understand the value of, and cover provided by, each benefit in order that they can make an appropriate selection.

It is unlikely that employees will understand flexible benefits properly when the concept is first discussed. It is therefore critical to invest time and resources in a full communications programme which offers sufficient information support, advice and feedback on an individual basis if necessary. It is also essential to listen to employees' reactions and to consult with them on their views.

¶226 Can I make the proposed flexible benefits plan compulsory?

Yes, but you should proceed cautiously if it is clear that some employees are not keen. The first step should be to try to introduce the flexible benefits plan by agreement. Remember that you may be able to 'buy' agreement by making some improvement in terms conditional on the employees accepting the flexible benefits plan. An obvious example would be to time the introduction of flexible benefits to coincide with the annual pay increase. Employees who do not accept the flexible benefits plan would forgo the increase.

An alternative, particularly if an organisation needs to introduce flexible benefits for cost reasons, is to hold down existing salaries, such that pay rises in effect are not reintroduced until the benefits are 'paid for' on the new basis.

If some employees still refuse, and there are good business reasons which make it important to the company that they should join the plan, they can as a last resort be dismissed and offered re-employment on the basis of the new plan. There are obvious risks with this approach, and legal advice should be

¶226

obtained before implementing it, but, if the company can show it acted reasonably (that is in accordance with good industrial relations practice), the dismissals should be fair.

In some circumstances organisations have introduced flex for those employees willing to join the scheme, and red-circled those employees remaining on the current benefits, until such time as the employee can buy the same benefits in the new plan.

¶227 Can I introduce flexible benefits into a unionised company?

Yes. Obviously the matter will have to be negotiated through the appropriate consultative procedure and it will be necessary to amend the relevant collective agreements, but, provided the unions are co-operative, being unionised is likely to be an advantage. The unions will help convince employees who might otherwise have wavered.

In different circumstances, if it is necessary to prove that a plan can be attractive, it may be appropriate to phase introduction, with the first plan designed for senior management.

¶228 What do I do if my employees do not want to join the flexible benefits plan?

Your next steps will depend on why you wanted to introduce flexible benefits. If you required a specific change, such as enrolling employees in a new pension scheme; or ceasing certain benefits, such as mortgage benefits, you could impose the plan (see ¶226). However, if you had other objectives for the plan, you might waive or delay your decision. Alternatively, you might offer optional enrolment to employees who are interested, and encourage a wider membership when the plan is in place.

In some circumstances it may be appropriate to offer incentives to encourage employees to change.

¶229 Do I need to change my existing employment contracts?

You will certainly need to review whether the existing contracts are appropriate. The terms of the flexible benefits plan will replace the corresponding terms of the contracts of employment. You will have to either draw up new contracts and ask employees to agree them or vary the old contracts by incorporating the new terms. See Chapter 12 for more detailed advice on this.

¶230 How do I administer a flexible benefits plan?

Administration is an important issue and is covered in more depth in Chapter 14. Briefly, decisions need to be taken on:

- whether to use in-house or third party administrators;
- whether to use a manual or computerised system;
- whether a new system needs to be developed or whether one can be purchased;
- who is to do the administration, and what training they need;
- what procedures are necessary.

Once this has been done, the administration system and procedures can be put in place. It is important to plan ahead in making these decisions. For example, if the plan is to be extended at a later stage, it is important to know that the system can cope with the increased complexity.

If the administration arrangements are planned well and executed properly, flex plans are not the nightmare many fear. One of the keys to this is keeping the plan simple.

¶231 What can go wrong?

If the plan is not properly structured, where salary is sacrificed for benefits purposes employees could find themselves taxed on the value of the benefit *and* the salary forgone. In certain circumstances, employers could find themselves with a VAT liability and unexpected National Insurance contributions.

If benefits and likely take-up are not actuarially costed, any adverse take-up of benefits could be unexpectedly costly.

¶232 Do I need professional advice?

Yes. Taxation, legal and actuarial benefit consulting is critical to avoid costly pitfalls. You may also require assistance on the administration systems which are available, and advice on the communications and employee involvement issues from those who have experience of implementing plans elsewhere.

3 Flexible Benefits are About Choice

Executive summary
- Flexible benefits offer a choice to employers to manage costs, and to maximise the value of their reward packages.
- Flexible benefits offer employees a choice to select benefits which suit their life stages and lifestyles.
- There is a range of possible flexible benefits plans from a plan which offers little choice, through 'menu' or 'modular' approaches, to cash-only compensation.
- Despite the benefits of choice, administrative complexity, the tax regime, and the effect of employee selection on company costs, have all discouraged employers in the UK from adopting a flexible approach.

The hierarchy of choice offered by the various types of flexible benefits plans are shown in Figure 3.

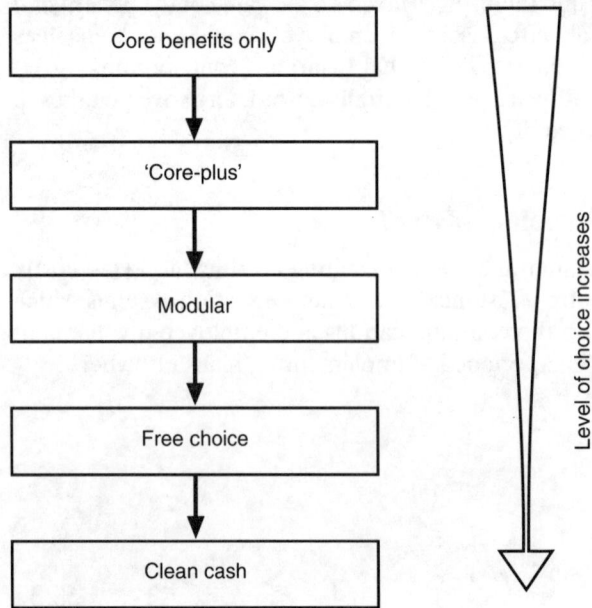

Figure 3: How much choice can we have?

¶301 Introduction

Flexible benefits, also known as 'flex', offer a choice both to employers and to employees. From the employer's perspective, flexible benefits plans can fulfil specific objectives, such as cost management, are tangible evidence of the corporate culture, and convey chosen messages to employees, particularly about status, innovation and personal responsibility.

From the employee's perspective, flexible benefits plans may allow a choice to suit particular life stages and lifestyles, and individual responsibility for the way in which remuneration is spent.

¶302 Choice (*chois*) n

In the context of flexible benefits 'choice' is usually taken to mean deciding between alternative benefits or ranges of benefits. However, a dictionary definition of the word choice is more extensive:

- a choosing or selection,
- the right or power to choose or an option,
- a person or thing chosen,
- the best part,
- a variety from which to choose,
- a supply well chosen,
- an alternative,
- care in choosing.

Of these, a choosing or selection, the right or power to choose, the best part, and care in choosing are all highly relevant to the flexible benefits approach.

¶303 Why do employers want to offer more choice?

Benefits cost a lot of money, and yet most employees think of their benefits package as fixed, and make comparisons between their own and others' remuneration on the basis of cash earned plus car.

Benefits can add from 10–15 per cent to salary costs for junior employees with a limited range of benefits, to 40–50 per cent for executives with more extensive benefits. In a few cases at the most senior levels benefits can cost as much as, or more than, the basic salary. In terms of the employee's perception of benefits, few employers achieve value for money from their benefits provision.

Giving employees a choice of benefits requires them to take an interest in the range of benefits in order for them to make an efficient choice (and they can only blame themselves if it is wrong) and take ownership of their choice. Also, employees understand better the value of each option when they are forced to make trade-offs. Together these activities provide an enhanced appreciation of the benefits package.

In all aspects of work, employees are recognising their organisations' increasing need for cost control. Flexible benefits plans allow the employer to share rising costs with employees without arbitrarily reducing the coverage of certain benefits, or increasing deductions from salary. The employer chooses how much to spend per employee, and so controls costs, but the employee can choose how to spend the available benefits money.

Flexible benefits packages in the UK are currently dominated by cars and pensions. This will continue to be the case while these benefits offer tax advantages. However, changes in the tax rules for cars combined with increasing costs to employers have led many to introduce alternatives to the standard company car. These include allowing employees to take a smaller car to lessen the tax burden or cash payments instead of a car.

In the UK, changes in pensions legislation have led some employers to review their pension arrangements in such a way that staff can make their own choices. The cap on pensionable earnings means that many companies are considering providing pensions promises without tax approval for affected employees. Such arrangements can only be made in a tax-inefficient way (a funded approach) or with some uncertainty for individuals (an unfunded approach). However, there is no one solution which will be right for everyone.

Less senior employees have also been offered choices in part because of the changes in pension legislation:

- occupational pension schemes can no longer insist on compulsory membership;
- employees have the right to opt out of SERPS;
- some employees can opt for a salary sacrifice whereby they accept a lower rate of future remuneration, but receive enhanced pension rights. In practice, however, salary sacrifice is less frequent than in previous years;
- contributors to all pension schemes have the right to make additional voluntary contributions;
- equalisation of retirement ages and benefits;
- proposed limited price indexation of pensions.

There are multiple incentives, therefore, pushing employers to offer more choice, from the external and legislative environment to their own need for cost control and pressure from employees.

¶303

¶304 Why do employees want more choice?

Before the recession, considerable attention was focused on demographic changes. Much was made of the need to attract women and older people back into the workforce. Despite job losses and recruitment bans, the profile of the workforce in the 1990s has changed. At all levels in business organisations the typical employee is no longer the middle aged male in a one income family with dependant children for whom many of our traditional remuneration packages are designed.

Employees in dual income families may find that their benefits overlap with their partner's. In these circumstances, contributions could usefully be diverted to providing different benefits. For example, those with dependants have additional needs in areas of care either for children or elderly relatives when both partners are at work.

There is also evidence that employees in the 1990s have a greater focus on quality of life. The option to increase leisure time or to pursue educational opportunities may these days be more attractive than the latest top of the range luxury car. Employees want flexible benefits and working conditions which will accommodate their family responsibilities.

Perhaps the most important of all is the recognition that employees' benefit needs change at different stages of life. A large life assurance policy has little perceived value for 20-year-olds renting their first flat. Older employees may wish, for example, to waive some of their car benefit to secure a better pension.

Very few truly flexible plans exist in the UK at present. However, as leading employers change their approach, and implement flexible packages, pressure will grow from employees for other employers to follow.

¶305 The scope for choice

Most employers in the UK offer some scope for choice *within* benefits, for example, the option to make additional voluntary contributions to pension, the option to take a smaller car, or to pay contributions towards a more expensive car. However, flexible benefits packages are also about choice *between* benefits, or the option to take more or less cash.

¶306 Choice between benefits

Figure 3 sets out different approaches to benefits provision from 'core', which offers little or no choice, to 'clean cash', which offers employees ultimate flexibility, since they receive no benefits in kind at all. We describe each of these options below:

- *Core benefits* provide little or no flexibility for employees. The employer determines what the employee will receive, and, in some instances, as with contributory pension schemes, what will be deducted from the employee's salary. Some core schemes do allow some flexibility within benefits, for example to cover a spouse and dependants in a medical care scheme, for which the employee contributes.

- *Core plus benefits* offer an employee a range of benefits which the employer offers as a minimum, usually for no contribution. In addition the employee can choose from a range of benefits up to a pre-set spending level. Most employers in the UK moving to a flexible approach choose core plus. In this way, they maintain their perceived social responsibility, since the core benefits are typically those related to the welfare of the employees and their families.

- *Modular benefits* offer employees a choice of benefit packages each containing a limited range of benefits; each module is tailored to appeal to different types of employee at different life stages.

- *Free choice* benefits offer even greater flexibility for each employee to choose, within a credit allocation or pre-set spending limit, the range and extent of benefits which suits his or her own personal circumstances.

- *Clean cash* can be expressed as offering either total or no flexibility; the employee can choose how to spend all his or her cash package, and with the suppliers he or she chooses. The employer, however, offers no benefit schemes. Despite the potential advantages – no benefits administration, accurate calculation of total compensation costs, and ease of market comparison – very few UK employers have followed this route. Whilst companies in many sectors are trying to move away from traditional cultures, few are brave enough to relinquish their perceived welfare responsibility (at least at a minimum level). Whether this results from a genuine concern for employees or from fear of adverse press, is unknown. Employers may also have a concern that applicants may compare a total cash package unfavourably with a cash plus benefits package offered by competitors during the recruitment process. The drawback for the employee is that clean cash attracts income tax and National Insurance contributions on the total package.

¶307 Choice in paying for benefits

In addition to choice between benefits and the way in which they are packaged, employers can also offer choice through the way in which benefits are paid. Some employers allow employees to make additional contributions to buy the desired level of benefit if this is not available from their standard credit.

A few employers also allow bonus sacrifice. If the employee elects to take certain benefits before the amount of bonus is determined, he or she will not pay tax on the cash he or she would have received, but will be taxed on the benefits he or she receives, or not taxed if they are tax-free as is the case with approved pension schemes.

¶308 Why not flexible benefits?

A survey by consultants Noble Lowndes highlights the low incidence of plans in the UK, and sought reasons for this. Of their respondents, 89 per cent said that a change in the tax regime would prompt their organisations to consider introducing flexible benefits.

Nevertheless, it seems that if an organisation's competitors were to introduce a plan, it would do likewise. Interestingly there is no correlation between the size of the companies which have introduced plans to date. Rather, certain sectors such as financial services or organisations with US parents have a greater prevalence of plans, suggesting that there is a 'me-too' attitude towards such plans.

¶309 If choice is so wonderful, why are there so few plans in operation in the UK?

Most companies which have recently considered, yet decided not to implement, flexible benefit packages cite three major reasons:

- the administrative complexity,
- the tax implications,
- the possibility of adverse selection.

These are discussed in turn below.

(1) Administrative complexity

With flexible benefits plans still in their infancy in the UK, few packages (computerised or manual) have been developed to support the administrative changes in benefits provision. US packages, even when tailored to meet individual requirements of UK companies, were historically unsuitable, and, until recently, the low volume of schemes had not encouraged potential providers to produce UK-specific packages. This situation is now changing, and, in Chapter 14, we review some of the options available.

(2) Tax implications

The tax regime until recently had favoured the provision of cars. The Inland Revenue used to treat a choice of cash or benefit in kind as creating a tax liability on the higher of the cash offered and the value of the benefit. For a time, Customs & Excise tried to assert that offering a choice created a VAT liability.

The fiscal climate has now changed. From April 1994, the tax treatment of a

22 Flexible Benefits

car, whether used for business or not, will be much closer to the tax treatment of its cash value.

The Inland Revenue takes a more realistic attitude to the treatment of cash alternatives and Customs & Excise's attempts to collect VAT where a cash alternative was offered in lieu of a car were trounced by both the VAT tribunal and the Chancellor.

Tax cannot be ignored, but is not an insuperable hurdle. We highlight the main issues in Chapter 11.

(3) Adverse selection

Adverse selection concerns employers because, if a significant number of employees opt out of a particular benefit, it can affect the costs for the employer for those staff who do wish to select the benefit. This is particularly true for insurance-related benefits where the age and sex profile of take-up can alter premium levels significantly. One way to influence choice is the way in which benefits are priced, both to encourage or discourage take up. This issue is explored in Chapter 8.

¶310 The benefit of choice

For the employer, the provision of choice and flexibility can give an employer a competitive advantage in the labour market. In addition, the precise targeting of benefits means that for any given level of employee cost, the value to the individual is maximised. Furthermore for any given level of value to the individual, the cost to the employer is minimised. Flexibility therefore offers an economic and efficient approach to all parties.

Perhaps the important issue is that, despite the complexities and difficulties, from the employee's perspective *choice in itself is considered a benefit*.

¶311 Flex: an example

Our next case study illustrates how a major US utilities company introduced Flex and has, as a consequence, gained a number of organisational advantages by offering benefits choice to its employees.

Case Study 2: Public Service Electric and Gas Company and flexible benefits

Public Service Electric and Gas Company (PSE&G), was founded in 1902. It was initially a utilities company spread around New Jersey, USA, and is now diversifying into other industries and countries around the world. It employs around 13,000 people, a large number of whom are union members.

PSE&G introduced flexible benefits, or Flex as it is called, in 1988. At the time the main reason for doing so was cost reduction, however, Flex has become an increasingly important tool for PSE&G over the years and while cost control continues to be an issue, other organisational benefits are now equally important to PSE&G.

Flex: reflecting the corporate culture of employee welfare
PSE&G's Flex plan focuses on the welfare of its employees and their changing needs and lifestyles. It is designed to give employees the ability to take control of their welfare planning in an environment that balances choice with corporate care. It includes, for example, dental and medical costs, long-term care protection for employees, their spouses and parents, life assurance, pensions and savings plans, and extended vacations. A more recent benefit was introduced giving employees reduced prices at a network of local pharmacies – demonstrating the ability to harness the buying power of the workforce in a way that individuals could not hope to achieve on their own.

Flex: helping to overcome employee resistance to changes in terms and conditions
When PSE&G first decided to introduce Flex it encountered significant resistance from the unions. The need to introduce Flex arose primarily from a need to control the cost of the Blue Cross private medical care plan. The plan was not only very generous, but, as a secondary issue, employees associated their medical protection with Blue Cross rather than seeing it as something that the company was providing – thus PSE&G had gained no value in their employees' eyes for such a generous level of cover.

The union members refused to agree to changes in their contracts and so initially the plan was only introduced for non-union members.

The change from Blue Cross that the company intended was a dramatic step to take and unfortunately took the focus away from the benefits of introducing Flex and what was being offered within the plan as a whole. It took some time to recover from that difficult start, but Flex soon came to be seen as a positive benefit for employees. Indeed, as the plan was extended over the next few years, it became so popular that union members actually asked to join rather than having to be coerced into doing so.

In 1993, PSE&G was able to introduce a second plan for its union members. The process for doing this was one of the first opportunities that management and unions had had to discuss a proposal that was seen as being beneficial to both parties and this helped build more positive relationships for other issues.

Flex: adding power to employee communications
From the first, PSE&G had learned the need to communicate effectively with employees so that the negative reactions which may arise could be

Flexible Benefits

minimised. The company put together a video and an introductory manual with lots of visual presentations and examples for employees to view in their own homes and discuss with their families. It is often the case that a spouse based at home has a better idea of the type and level of medical and life assurance cover that is necessary for the family, than a working spouse. Included in the pack were ready reckoners to help individuals to see clearly what levels of benefit they would gain for each dollar allocated.

That said, it was not all plain sailing and the company was thwarted by, among other things, the vagaries of the mail system. Some people did not get their presentation package on time and others did not get it at all – which caused problems of its own.

The communication systems that have been built up to give employees the necessary details to take informed decisions are part of an overall plan of employee communications across the organisation. For its Flex plan, PSE&G focused its thinking on the information that needed to be communicated, and how this was to be done. The company's efforts have been acknowledged by industrial awards given for some of its publications. It is not possible here to illustrate the visual form of the communications or the innovative methods PSE&G has employed to be effective in what it has to say, but some of the ways PSE&G does this are:

- *'Spectrum'*: a benefits newsletter to provide timely information about the benefits that are available and details on any new benefits being introduced.
- *Benefits annual report*: a summary of all the benefits available over the last year with financial information showing the cost to the company of providing their share of the benefits and including a poster setting out the options available for the coming year structured to reflect the changing lifestyles of employees.
- *Summary plan descriptions*: comprehensive summaries of the benefits.
- *Take home planning video and brochure*: tools given to those employees attending a financial planning seminar so that they can consider their choices at home with their families. The planning ideas are specifically long term – helping employees to focus on why they need financial planning, and how to make decisions in the short term.
- *Summary brochure for retirees*: a guide to the options that retiring employees can continue to take part in to help them understand any decisions that they may have to make regarding their pensions.

Flex: using technology to take the strain
Capturing the choices of some 13,000 employees who elect once a year for their benefit coverage is a potentially daunting task. Time has to be allowed

¶311

to enable the company to collate the choices, to deal with those who fail to respond (and there will always be some who are automatically entered as taking minimum cover on all benefits) to arrange the various plans externally, and then to implement the decisions.

PSE&G has an interactive telephone system for the collection of the information. Employees ring in to a computer linked to the company's mainframe and are guided by the programme into giving the necessary information. There are automatic checks to prevent any invalid information being loaded.

For the current year PSE&G is adding a benefit administration record keeping system. Computers will be installed in 70 locations around the country. Employees will then input, with the help of user-friendly touch screens, all their personal information and any changes to it which will automatically be down-loaded onto the company's mainframe and linked directly into its HR systems. The data on benefits will be stored externally by administrators in order to avoid too much of the company's own computer capacity being used. With this system, employees can not only input their required benefits but, at any time in the year, can also get summaries of their chosen benefits which are often necessary if their personal circumstances change. All this without the need to tie up the personnel department's time.

Flex: a tool for retaining and motivating
In summary, PSE&G is committed to its Flex plan, and each year adds new benefits that give employees the chance to share in the company's buying power, and at the same time puts in place the necessary welfare provisions to give employees peace of mind. By being innovative in this fashion, PSE&G knows that it has the opportunity to attract the right people to the organisation and to retain them – while at the same time controlling the increasing costs of so doing.

¶311

4 Why Flexible Benefits? – Setting Objectives

Executive summary
- The motives for flexible benefits differ significantly between the US and the UK. The issues which made organisations consider, but not introduce, flex a few years ago are once more relevant in the UK as it emerges from the recession.
- Cost management is a major consideration for many UK companies considering flex.
- Specific, measurable objectives should be set for the flex project as a baseline for the pricing and costing stages in the design loop (Figure 2).
- It will be necessary to revisit the objectives and to refine or realign them throughout the project.

¶401 Motives for flexible benefits

In the US, many employers introduced flexible benefits plans because of the escalating cost of medical insurance. The new plans offer the chance to move away from the old-style health and retirement plans which promised specific benefits, to plans where the employers' contribution and costs are fixed. The other major reason for introduction, recruitment and retention of staff, took flexible benefits off the agenda during the recession as organisations focused their cost control efforts on their major business operations and headcount reductions. However, as we emerge from the economic constraints of the recession, the human resource management issues will once again become important, these include:

- demographics and the workforce profile,
- hot competition for fewer high-quality staff,
- catching up on recruitment cutbacks,
- reward for different and flexible skills sets.

Insurance costs are rising in the UK, although not to the extent that they have in the US. Nevertheless, fringe benefits are no longer marginal to the overall compensation package. Such benefits represent a major cost and cost control is the reason most organisations give for their interest in flexible benefits.

¶402 Stated objectives

Figure 4 sets out the objectives reported in a recent study by organisations as to their own benefits priorities now and in the future.

Priority	Current	Future
1	Controlling benefit costs	Controlling benefit costs
2	Reducing benefit administration costs	Recruiting and retaining staff
3	Recruiting and retaining staff	Improving the match between the benefit package and corporate objectives/business plans
4	Improving the match between the benefit package and corporate objectives/business plans	Improving the match between the benefit package and the evolving workforce
5	Improving the match between the benefit package and the evolving workforce	Managing employees' perceptions of benefits
6	Managing employees' perceptions of benefits	Reducing benefit administration costs
7	Reducing benefit costs in general	Reacting to the impact of UK/EC legislative changes
8	Reacting to the impact of UK/EC legislative changes	Reducing benefit costs in general

Source: Towers Perrin, 'The Benefits Package of the Future' (October 1992)

Figure 4: Current and future benefit priorities

¶403 Some example objectives

Although the introduction of flexible benefits should not be a knee-jerk reaction to increased labour turnover or staff demands, the organisation's financial health, philosophy and culture will influence the objectives. Many current benefits packages have developed over the years as a result of economic pressures, such as the restraints on cash pay in the 1970s, and attempts to match competitor packages.

There have been a number of surveys by academics and consultants in the last two years to sound out employers' interest in and reservations about flexible benefits. In addition to the priorities in Figure 4, other objectives quoted for consideration or introduction of flexible benefits are to:

- keep benefits costs within sector/national average;
- focus on the cost of total compensation;
- remove commitment to match rising costs;
- increase tax efficiency (corporate and individual);
- make savings in employer's National Insurance contributions, since NIC is payable on salary, but not on many benefits in kind;
- attract best talent;
- increase the value of compensation packages at little or no added company expense;
- offset changes in existing benefits such as restrictions to the car scheme;
- reward key executives;
- improve employee morale;
- develop consistency in benefits worldwide or in Europe to facilitate staff transfers;
- reinforce or change the corporate culture;
- move from paternalism to individual responsibility;
- integrate benefits packages on merger or acquisition;
- equalise status-related benefits;
- phase out a particular benefit;
- increase or decrease take up of a particular benefit;
- link benefits provision to corporate or individual performance.

In practice, those organisations which have introduced flexible benefits have done so because they want to make a specific change. For example, two companies in the financial services sector wanted to move staff to a new pension scheme. The introduction of a flexible benefits package provided the motivation for staff to accept the change.

¶404 The need for objectives

As with any project, it is important to set objectives for the introduction of a flexible benefits plan so that the organisation can set criteria in order to assess its success.

In many cases these criteria will include the cost of current packages which may need to be calculated especially for this exercise.

¶405 An opportunity to reconsider objectives

The introduction of a new package allows an organisation to consider what it wants to achieve from its benefits package, and to design a new plan which fits the corporate goals and ethos. In an ideal world organisations would follow this process. In practice, however, many organisations decide they want to move to a flexible benefits approach, and then set the objectives. In any case, the objectives will be shaped by the answer to three fundamental questions:

- Do we need flexible benefits at all?
- What are the cost constraints?
- Which employee groups will be included in the plan or plans?

¶406 The need to revisit objectives

Figure 2 illustrates the need to revisit the objectives for flex at different stages of the project. It is likely that objectives will be refined or even changed as an organisation, in the light of greater knowledge about flex, recognises whether the objectives are appropriate or sustainable. Our third case study shows how one company responded to changes in its organisational priorities.

Case Study 3: A financial services organisation – the need for objectives
Over the last ten years, each of the industries in the financial services sector has been transformed by major regulatory, structural and economic influences. Alongside changes to the industry structure has come a focus on human resources management, with new policies to reflect this change in emphasis. The case study organisation is such a company.

A flexible benefits policy would have been at the forefront of human resources practice in the investment banking sector. To introduce such a policy would signal to employees the company's commitment to attracting and retaining the best staff in the industry by providing a benefits package to suit individual needs.

Amongst other human resources initiatives at this time was a review of pensions arrangements and the company was anxious that employees should switch to the new pension plan. A flexible benefits plan was seen as an attractive vehicle to ensure new pension arrangements would be received positively by employees.

In the early stages, the company identified other benefits arising from the flex approach:

- improved cost control;

- greater flexibility;
- increased moral, motivation and commitment;
- responsibility for planning to meet lifestyle needs;
- increased awareness of the cost of benefit provision;
- business unit accountability.

However, research on the feasibility of a flexible benefits plan, and the potential design, raised a number of issues which challenged the original basis for its introduction, for example:

- Did improved cost control imply that the new benefits scheme should cost less than current benefit provisions, cost no more or simply ensure that future increases should be more tightly controlled?
- It was decided that anomalies would be eliminated by allowing some staff to end up better off under the scheme. How should the company respond to the consequent increase in costs?
- To what levels of staff would flexibility be provided, and would it then be appropriate to sell flexibility as an additional benefit if some staff were excluded?
- What would be the effect on motivation and morale if the scheme were designed around the organisational hierarchy, and some benefits continued to be status driven related to seniority or salary level?
- How should the company reconcile differences in culture within the organisation such that, for example, employees in one section might welcome the opportunity to optimise the purchasing potential of their benefit package while those in another preferred to leave choices to the company?
- The age profile of the employees raised concern about the effects on insurance premiums if only those who felt they were at risk opted for insured benefits (for further discussion on this issue, see Chapter 8).

As the plan was developed, objectives changed to reflect the company's desire to seek fair and equitable solutions and its concern to manage the challenges of a major change in the approach to benefits. In the event, the company decided to introduce a limited flex restricted to pensions and company cars for all eligible employees. The package included an element of flexibility, allowing managers to top up some benefits which the company provided as core. The company intends to phase the introduction of flexible benefits so that a wider range of benefits will be offered in the future.

The case study shows how the objectives of a flexible benefit plan are refined. They are initially established against the overall business objectives;

they are then tested against the business climate, and against the level of change the corporate culture will accept. As the case study illustrates, these objectives may well shift as the design process flushes out those issues which are relevant to benefits practice and which influence the corporate culture.

5 Costing the Current Benefits Package

Executive summary
- It is critical to understand how much the existing benefits package costs before starting to develop a flex plan to provide a baseline against which to measure the cost or saving of introducing flex. This is the second step shown in the design loop (Figure 2).
- All the benefits, including those which may not be included in the flex plan, must be costed.

¶501 Establish a cost baseline

Many organisations consider introducing flexible benefits in order to:

- reduce costs, or
- control costs.

In other cases, organisations want to introduce a new benefit profile which costs the same as the existing package, that is, a cost-neutral plan. However, in practice, very few have an accurate picture of the cost of current benefits. In order to achieve any of the cost goals, it is critical to establish a baseline from which to measure.

¶502 Understanding the current cost

Somewhat surprisingly many organisations do not know how much their current benefits package costs. This is because frequently different elements are administered in different parts of the organisation and through different budgets. For example, the personnel department manages life assurance and the car fleet vehicle provision, and the company secretary administers the pension scheme. In large organisations, responsibility for costs may be devolved to local departments which each keep their own records.

Flexible benefit plans force a more cohesive approach to managing benefit costs and an important first step in this direction should be an analysis of the costs of all elements of the current benefits package.

A further consideration is whether to cost:

- the benefits policy, or
- the benefits practice.

If, for example, private medical care is available for all staff, should you calculate the cost on that basis, or should you calculate on the basis of actual take-up? Similarly, should a financial services company which offers a preferential mortgage arrangement cost the benefit for all those who fit the age and length of service criteria, irrespective of whether they currently take advantage of the benefit?

In most cases, it is probably appropriate to cost the benefits practice, since this represents the actual cost to the organisation.

At this stage, you need do no more than add up the total cost of providing each benefit offered in the flex plan. In Chapter 8, we describe the further analysis involved in developing a pricing system based on the cost of existing benefits.

¶503 What to include

Organisations generally find it a useful exercise to include all benefits, even if it is unlikely that several of them would be included in a flex package. This approach facilitates a better management understanding of the total cost of employing each member of staff. It may also provide the data necessary to communicate total benefit values to staff.

It is also instructive to collect cost data for all grades (even if some will not be covered in a flex plan) as this will give a good understanding of the relativities between the total packages at different levels.

¶504 Analysing the data

At this early stage, when it is unlikely that an organisation is fully committed to develop a flex plan it is best to keep any analysis simple, thus the framework in Figure 5 should probably suffice.

Benefit	A £	A %	B £	B %	C £	C %	D £	D %	Total £	Total %
Car	8,000	8.0	6,000	12.0	4,000	13.3	3,000	15.0	21,000	10.5
Pension	25,000	25.0	7,500	15.0	4,500	15.0	2,000	10.0	39,000	19.5
Life assurance	3,000	3.0	1,000	2.0	600	2.0	400	2.0	5,000	2.5
Long-term disability	1,500	1.5	500	1.0	300	1.0	200	1.0	2,500	1.3
Personal accident	500	0.5	250	0.5	150	0.5	100	0.5	1,000	0.5
Subsidised canteen	250	0.3	120	0.2	120	0.4	120	0.6	610	0.3
Total	38,250	38.3	15,370	30.7	9,670	32.2	5,820	29.1	69,110	34.6
Salary	100,000		50,000		30,000		20,000		200,000	

Figure 5: Costing the current benefits

The figures in the '£' column would normally be the total of the costs for each benefit in a particular grade. Wherever possible the cost and salary grade figures should have similar effective dates (for example, both are reviewed on 1 January each year).

Apart from pension, these figures should generally include the cash costs of the benefits taken up by staff. Some benefits, such as disability and life insurance, are typically salary related and, for these, assuming all staff in a grade have the same benefit, the figures in the '£' column can be derived by applying a known percentage to the total salaries in that grade. In the case of pensions the best figure to use might be the regular cost used for determining pension costs in the audited accounts as this will not be affected by contribution holidays.

The figures in the '%' column can be derived from the ratio of total benefit costs in a grade to total salaries, or total cash remuneration.

This cost analysis is the starting point to provide a framework to define cost requirements for the new plan. For example, an organisation may wish to reduce benefit costs from 30 per cent of salary to 25 per cent of salary over a period of five years.

¶504

6 Designing the Plan – The Key Parameters

Executive summary

- Step 2 in the design loop (Figure 2) is to revisit the objectives for the flex plan, and to set the design parameters, which will include how many employees, and which benefits will be covered by the plan.
- At this stage, the employer will decide how much flexibility to build into the plan, and how frequently employees may change their selection of benefits.
- An important design criteria is whether employees will be given a monetary value or a notional points credit to spend on benefits.

¶601 The importance of objectives – revisited

The objectives of the organisation should be reflected in the plan design. For example, a wish to 'ensure all staff have a better appreciation of their benefits package' can only be achieved if all staff are in the plan. Similarly, an aim to 'encourage staff to transfer to a new pension plan' will only be achieved if the pension plan is linked to the flex plan in some way. These are obvious examples, but it is very easy to forget the main reasons for introducing flexible benefits when it comes to putting the plan together.

The organisation's culture will also define what is and is not acceptable in a plan. For example, a single-status company is unlikely to be comfortable with a flex plan that distinguishes between staff and management.

¶602 Design parameters

It is possible to reach decisions fairly quickly on the outline of the design, for example which people and which benefits should be included. However, the design can only be finalised once each of the options have been priced, credit allowances have been set and the introduction of the plan costed. The principle parameters which need to be decided at the outset are:

- eligibility;
- scope of choice;
- benefits to be included;
- timing of elections; and
- currency of pricing.

It is worthwhile emphasising that the structure of the plan will only be complete once prices have been determined for each benefit and a 'credit allowance' has been set. This is the amount which an individual has to spend on the benefits on offer. In most cases, an addition to cash salary will arise if there are unspent credits and a reduction in or deduction from salary if excess benefits are chosen. The tax implications of a reduction in and deduction from salary in lieu of benefits are discussed in Chapter 11 and Appendix 2. Where a reduced salary is taken the question of what constitutes salary for, say, pension purposes arises. This is also discussed in Appendix 2 in relation to the true or notional salaries.

¶603 Eligibility

Under non-flexible arrangements, the availability or level of many benefits will probably be grade or seniority driven. Typically, senior executives enjoy greater pension and life assurance cover than other managers, and, in many organisations, cars and private health care are only provided from middle manager level upwards.

Although the introduction of a flexible benefits plan offers the opportunity to move away from reward for status, it is important not to underestimate the cultural resistance which may exist towards such an egalitarian approach. Some organisations may prefer an approach which signals significant cultural change, others an approach which fits well with the current culture. The possible options for plan eligibility are:

- All employees will be eligible on similar terms.
- All employees will be eligible, but benefits credits will be related to salary, usually expressed as a percentage. In this type of plan, the benefits package continues to reflect status to some extent.
- All employees will be eligible, but certain benefits will be reserved for certain grades of management or salary levels.
- Separate plans will be introduced for different employee populations, so that benefits continue to reflect seniority and status.

The employer will also need to decide whether implementation of the plan will be phased in. For example, an organisation which wants to introduce an all-employee scheme may implement a limited plan first for senior staff, to introduce the concept of flexibility to the culture, and to learn from the design and implementation process.

¶604 Scope for choice

Chapter 3 outlines the types of choice which can be built into the plan. At this stage, the organisation needs to decide which of the following it will use for each of the plans to be introduced:

- core benefits,
- core plus,
- modular,
- free choice,
- clean cash.

As discussed, objectives of the plan and the culture of the organisation will decide how great a degree of choice the organisation wishes to offer its employees.

Although logically one would expect the employee to be entitled to decide what he or she gets within the plan rules, in some cases, the employer retains the right to override an employee's decision if the administrators of the plan consider the employee's choice inappropriate. Whilst this may offer the employer some comfort, in our view, it mitigates against the concept of choice, and calls into question the design of the plan.

Some organisations nervous of a 'big bang' approach, and which do not want to introduce full flexibility at a stroke, have found advantages in phasing the introduction. The first stages might allow employees to flex a narrow range of benefits while remaining benefits are provided as before. If the implementation goes well, and regular monitoring shows that the plan is successful, new benefits can be included at subsequent renewals.

¶605 Benefits to be included

To some extent the benefits to be included will reflect the type of choice an organisation has decided to offer. A core-plus approach indicates that the organisation has determined the core benefits which it considers are essential for every employee to have.

Organisations which take this approach typically include a minimum level of life cover, pension, holiday, long-term disability and, perhaps, medical insurance. The welfare nature of these benefits reflects the responsibility many employers take on for their employees.

¶605

A less paternalistic organisation may not feel the need to provide basic cover, and will therefore offer a free choice from a long list of benefits.

Figure 6 lists the benefits which might be included in a flexible benefits plan. In addition, it is important to decide whether cash will be included as a benefit, that is, employees who do not wish to use their full benefit entitlement may receive additional cash.

Mainstream	Interesting add-ons
Car	Counselling (financial, legal)
Pension	Child care vouchers
Life assurance	Retail vouchers
Disability cover	Personal accident
Medical insurance	Dental insurance
Annual leave	Optical insurance
Share options	Dental scheme
Private petrol	Sports clubs
Mortgage subsidy	Computer equipment purchase
Loans	Sabbaticals
	School fee assistance
	Language training
	Car parking
	Credit card subscriptions
	Membership fees
	Clothing allowances

Figure 6: Possible benefits for inclusion

Whether pensions should be included in the flexible package often causes considerable debate. The discussion is most frequently not about whether it is appropriate to include pensions, but about the difficulties associated with pricing the benefits in the new plan, and costing the impact of partial take-up.

Chapter 7 considers the key issues surrounding the inclusion of some of the major benefits in the new plan, including pensions.

¶606 Timing of elections

A further parameter to consider in the design of the new benefits package is how frequently members of the plan may change their elections. Each time employees elect, or change their election, the take-up of benefits will alter, and there will be an administration cost. The election periods most frequently used are:

- annual;
- annual to coincide with salary award;
- to coincide with expiry of car lease arrangements, about three to four years.

In addition, most plans allow a further election when there is a major change in the employee's life, including marriage, birth of a child, divorce or a death in the family.

¶607 Currency of pricing or credits

Credits are the notional allocation given to employees to 'buy' the benefit options of their choice. The option prices and credit allowances can be expressed in terms of monetary amounts or points.

Advantage for the monetary approach are:

- It clearly communicates the value of benefits to staff and management.
- It is simple and transparent.

On the other hand, advantages for a points system are:

- Adjustments in the pricing system can be hidden (although an exchange rate from points to pounds will usually exist, and it is therefore difficult to hide very much).
- Points can be weighted to either encourage or discourage take up of a particular benefit.
- Points can be more user friendly.
- Prices expressed in points might remain stable from year to year while the value of a point is changed (although this can be constraining if staff come to expect the relative values within the plan to remain constant).
- Adjustments can be made to take account of National Insurance contributions.
- Administration costs can be included in the points allocation.

It will normally also be possible for some, or all, of the credit to be turned into additional salary.

¶608 Plan design – some examples

Figure 7 sets out the outline design for an example plan. In this company there is a two-tier core plus system:

- Multi flex for all staff earning £45,000 and above;
- Flex tier for all staff earning between £25,000 – £45,000.

Flex tier: salary £25,000–£45,000 per annum

Benefit	Core benefit	Top up level
Life assurance	2 × £30,000	3 × £30,000 4 × £30,000
Private medical insurance	Single, Band C	Bands: A or B Cover: married, etc.
Pension scheme	Employer's contribution: 10% of salary	Employer's contribution: 30% of salary
Permanent health insurance	33.3% of £30,000 plus 5% escalating	66.6% of £30,000 plus 5% escalating

Multi flex: salary above £45,000 per annum
Flex tier plus the following:

Benefit	Top up level
Car	Choice
Personal accident insurance	5 × £30,000
Personal financial planning	Gold service (2 hour) Diamond service (5 hour plus tax return)
Child care vouchers	Total choice of child care provision
Dental and optical insurance	National plan
Dental care	Annual check up, hygienist X-ray and discounts
Health/fitness	Local clubs
Educational scheme	Managed funds
Sabbaticals	Bank points for full/part payment

Exclusions:

Annual leave	Employee assistance	Medical screening
Bonus scheme	Share schemes	Luncheon vouchers
Company sick pay	Interest-free ticket loans	Subsidised mortgage

Figure 7: An example benefit plan

¶608

Designing the Plan – The Key Parameters

All employees must take the core benefits. Once a year eligible employees are invited to select benefits from a top-up menu. Those in the multi flex are entitled to a greater number of the additional benefits than those in the flex tier. If employees choose more benefits than their allowance, they may make up the difference with a contribution from salary. As noted earlier, the tax implications of this contribution are explored in Appendix 2. Similarly, staff who do not use all their benefits allowance may receive an additional cash payment on top of their basic salary.

Figure 8 sets out an election form for a flexible benefits plan. The box at the top right hand corner shows the total credits available to the employee. Below are the benefits available with the cost of buying those benefits.

The employee selects the benefits required at the desired level and adds up the total amount spent. If there are any unused credits, these may be available as additional salary.

¶608

42 Flexible Benefits

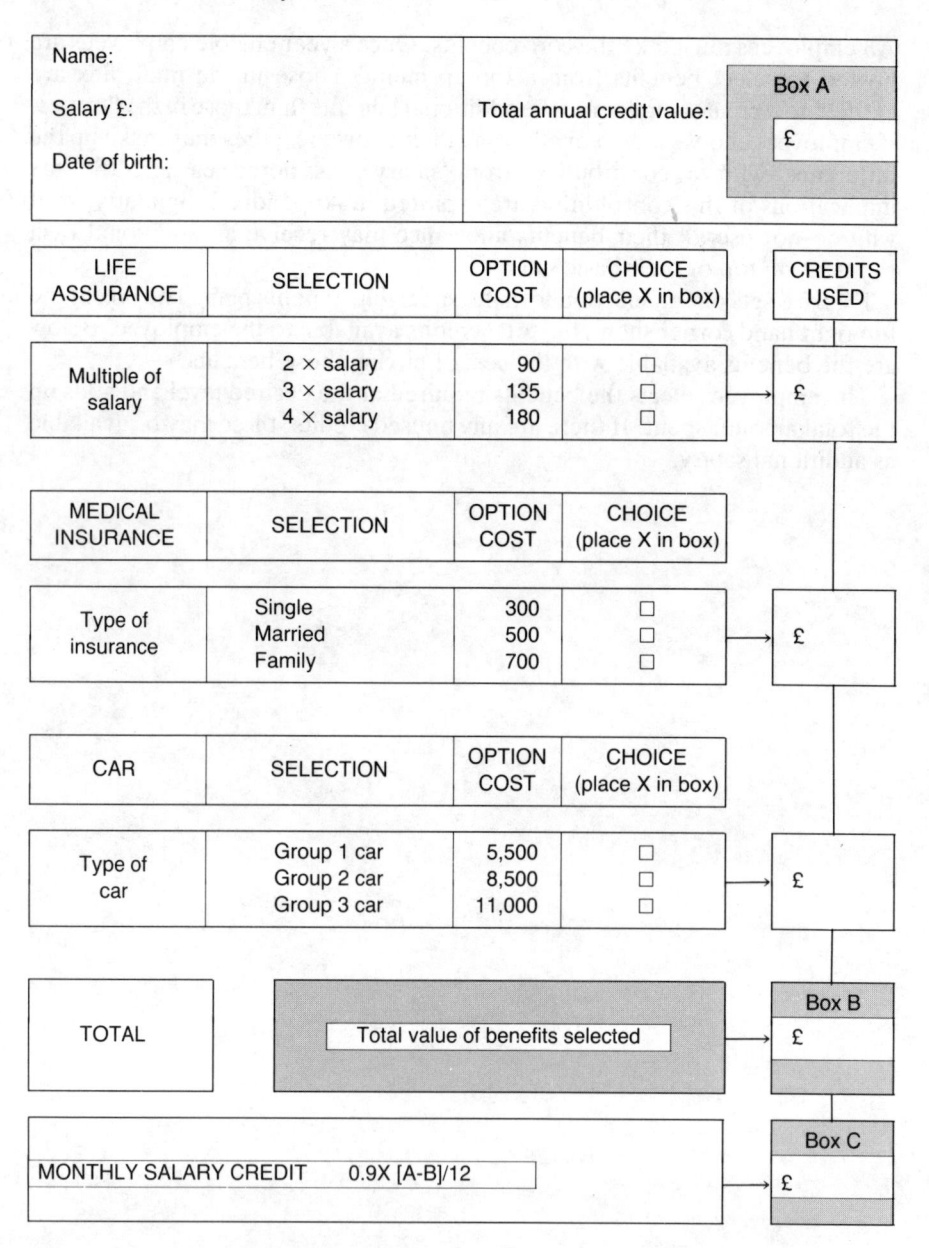

Name:		Box A
Salary £:	Total annual credit value:	£
Date of birth:		

LIFE ASSURANCE	SELECTION	OPTION COST	CHOICE (place X in box)	CREDITS USED
Multiple of salary	2 × salary 3 × salary 4 × salary	90 135 180	☐ ☐ ☐	£

MEDICAL INSURANCE	SELECTION	OPTION COST	CHOICE (place X in box)	
Type of insurance	Single Married Family	300 500 700	☐ ☐ ☐	£

CAR	SELECTION	OPTION COST	CHOICE (place X in box)	
Type of car	Group 1 car Group 2 car Group 3 car	5,500 8,500 11,000	☐ ☐ ☐	£

TOTAL	Total value of benefits selected	Box B £

MONTHLY SALARY CREDIT 0.9X [A-B]/12	Box C £

Figure 8: Scheme X flexible benefits plan – sample election form

¶608

7 Designing the Plan – The Major Benefits

Executive summary

- An important design parameter is which benefits to include in the flex plan.
- Many employers currently offer flexibility within the car benefit to take account of the erosion of tax advantages. Cash is becoming a more attractive alternative.
- It is more straightforward to incorporate a money purchase pension than a final salary pension into a flex plan because the cost of the plan is defined.
- The effect of employee take-up on all risk benefits within a flex plan can alter the cost to the employer, and impose restrictions on certain employee groups.
- It may not be appropriate for employees to opt out of risk benefits unless their spouse provides written consent.
- Holiday entitlement is frequently included in flex plans, usually up to a maximum limit.
- There are a number of other benefits typically included in flex plans.

¶701 Introduction

For each benefit to be included in the flex plan careful consideration needs to be given to the following:

- Any ethical issues the company will face by allowing freedom of choice. For example, are the company's moral obligations satisfied if employees are allowed to opt out of life assurance cover altogether?
- The question of 'whose benefit is it anyway?' for benefits which offer advantages to both employer and employee such as medical insurance and holiday entitlement.
- Any loss of group discount due to reduced numbers and insurers' loadings to cover additional risk.

- Options for each benefit need to be structured to allow for these issues as well as the fundamental aims of the plan.

Figure 6 sets out the wide range of benefits which can be included in a flex plan. Many of the benefits are relatively straightforward but those most commonly found in existing remuneration packages can present some difficult and often conflicting issues. The benefits are:

- a company car;
- pension;
- life assurance;
- medical insurance;
- long-term disability insurance; and
- holiday entitlement.

These benefits represent the bulk of the cost and value of most benefits packages and consequently will often be at the heart of a flex plan. This chapter explores the practical and ethical issues presented by introducing these benefits into a plan. The pricing of each benefit is explored in Chapter 8.

¶702 Company car

For many employees, the provision of a company car is a highly emotive subject. The 1980s saw a considerable increase in the provision of company cars as part of employees' benefit packages. This was as a result of wage restraint, demand from employees and the considerable tax advantages of providing such a benefit. However, these tax advantages have been considerably reduced by a succession of budgets in which the relative tax charge on company cars has been increased substantially. This reduction will undoubtedly have an impact on the attractiveness of company cars to many employees, leading them to demand greater choice both between cars at different price levels and between a car and cash.

(1) Including cars in flex plans

The inclusion of company cars in flex plans is a natural and often first step for many companies to take because personal tastes differ considerably and employees value a wide choice. At one extreme, some employees will be willing to sacrifice a significant part of their earnings to enable them to drive a more expensive car, whereas at the other, senior executives may be provided with cars that they consider to be inappropriately expensive and, given the choice, would choose a less expensive car and take extra earnings.

On the other hand, an employer may consider a certain type of car to be essential for an employee undertaking his business, although at the other extreme there may be a requirement that the company car is not too ostentatious.

Employers' attitudes towards company cars are changing: many consider their provision to be administratively burdensome and inordinately time consuming. It is likely that company car fleets will be substantially reduced in coming years.

(2) Structuring options

The structure of options offered to employees regarding company cars will depend to some extent on how the car scheme operates at present, and how much administration the company is willing to bear. Examples of possible approaches are:

- A range of benchmark cars is offered, each with a specified price tag. Each benchmark car would have a group of alternative models attached. For cost control purposes, these alternative models could be selected to be cheaper than the benchmark car itself. Benchmark cars may be set for each grade of employee with the option to trade up if a contribution is paid from their salary.
- A limited range of cars is offered, each with a price tag.
- An unlimited range of cars is offered, each with a price tag.
- A combination of the benchmark approach and individual pricing. Generally a standard range of vehicles are grouped into a benchmark system. If an employee requests a car outside this range, it will be individually priced, perhaps at a premium.

(3) Restricting choice

The inclusion of company cars within a flexible benefits plan means that options can only be exercised when each employee's car lease term expires. This may be contrary to total flexibility from the employees' viewpoint.

Organisations are increasingly seeking to restrict employees' choice with regard to company cars. For example, cars which have a higher level of depreciation or which are particularly susceptible to car theft are often excluded from company car fleet lists. These limitations can be incorporated in a flex plan or differential pricing can be used to discourage employees from making certain choices, or at least to ensure that the administrative costs are covered.

The employer will need to take account of the possibility that employees might leave before the end of a car lease period. In such instances, the company would then incur surrender penalties, or be left with a relatively unmarketable car which may be inappropriate to the car fleet, but result in a significant loss upon disposal.

¶702

(4) Car or cash

Even employers who are not yet considering a full flexible benefits approach are offering employees the option of a cash allowance instead of a vehicle.

This has arisen because of changes to tax liabilities for the individual. Some employees are now in a position where they would be better off financially buying or leasing their own vehicle.

Initially, the option to take cash caused a debate between employers and Customs & Excise about potential VAT liabilities. This matter has now been resolved in a way which makes the cash alternative more attractive to employers and employees. Nevertheless, offering cash in lieu of a car can create potential tax traps for both the company and the employee.

Appendix 1 sets out briefly the tax and contractual issues around the cars or cash option. CCH Editions' guide to the subject, *Car or Cash? A guide for employers and employees in making the choice*, explores the matter more fully, from both the employers' and employees' perspective.

¶703 Pension

Companies provide pension benefits for their employees in a number of ways. To consider how pension provision may be incorporated into a flexible benefits plan, it is necessary to distinguish between two distinct approaches: money purchase and final salary pension provision.

(1) Money purchase pensions

Money purchase pensions specify contribution rates to be paid by an employer and its employees. The contributions are invested in the pension arrangement on behalf of the employees and accumulate in accordance with the investment performance of the fund. It is a straightforward matter to incorporate a money purchase scheme into a flexible benefits plan, because the cost of the scheme is defined at the start. The options would normally be based on different specified levels of employer contribution, or perhaps a free choice up to a certain percentage of salary.

(2) Final salary pensions

In simple terms, a final salary pension scheme provides a pension which is the product of the salary earned by the individual up to the point of retirement, and not of the pension fund. Final salary pension schemes are more difficult to incorporate in a flexible benefits plan. This is partly a function of the company's contribution being variable to meet the ongoing funding requirements of the scheme. Further, a few pension schemes offer more than one level of benefit, and may even give the option to transfer from one section to another at specified times. However, it is more usual for benefits to be fixed at one level for the majority of employees. For the reasons given below, it is unlikely that a company will be able to offer different levels of final salary benefits in a flex plan, although there may be scope for additional employer contributions to be made on a money purchase basis.

The cost of providing a final salary pension is likely to be considerably more for an older employee than for a younger one. Indeed, the cost of providing that benefit for the oldest employee may well be more than twice the cost for the youngest employee. This makes it increasingly difficult to price different levels of final salary pension without seeming to penalise older staff at a time when they have a high level of awareness of their pension benefits.

Difficulties can also arise when a company has a pension contribution holiday. Structuring a realistic cash alternative can be problematic because any cash paid to an individual (or perhaps on an individual's behalf into a personal pension plan) will involve an increase in cash costs which is unlikely to be acceptable to most companies.

(3) Flex as an incentive

Figure 9 sets out an example of how pensions may be included in a flex plan. If care is taken, this can be a means of avoiding having to provide expensive pension guarantees.

As a result of several acquisitions a company was operating a number of final salary pension schemes. Along with the introduction of a flexible benefits plan, the company was keen to rationalise its pension arrangements. It recognised the difficulties in incorporating a final salary pension scheme within a flexible benefits plan but there was considerable resistance from the workforce to a change from final salary to money purchase pension provision.

The company successfully incorporated pensions within the flexible benefits plan by offering a core final salary pension benefit at a relatively modest level with pensions being based upon an accrual rate of $\frac{1}{80}$th. Employees could opt for higher levels of pension provision but the excess benefits are provided on a money purchase basis. The company was therefore able to achieve its main aims, namely:

- Rationalise its pension arrangements.
- Provide a core final salary pension benefit.
- Provide excess pension benefits under a money purchase basis, thereby simplifying the costing process.

Figure 9: Example of how pensions may be included in a flex plan

¶703

(4) Ethical issues

These days, very few people have a 'cradle-to-grave' career within one organisation, and thus the provision of a good pension is unlikely to have the same ethical dimension as it did for past generations. Many companies are now happy for employees to make their own provision for retirement while others are focusing their pension scheme arrangements on those who need and appreciate them most – those over 35 years of age. These features are easily incorporated into flex plans and, perhaps, point to eventual free choice on the level of pension provision. However, there are two issues which require careful thought:

- Whether a spouse's pensions will be adequate on an employee's death if the employee can choose his or her own pension level.
- Whether pension cover will be adequate to facilitate retirement or early retirement when the company requires it.

These points may lead to restrictions on choice to ensure that pension provision is adequate, or, regarding the first point, that the employee's spouse is required to sign any election forms.

(5) Inland Revenue limits

The Inland Revenue places limits on pension benefits and it is important that employees understand that these could apply. For example, with a money purchase scheme a contribution rate of 15 per cent may be on offer, but for younger staff this may be sufficient to fund benefits well in excess of the Inland Revenue's limits. In these circumstances an employee's choice may need to be overridden.

If, as in the case of a final salary scheme, options are structured on the basis of benefit levels rather than contributions, care must be taken not to promise more than can be provided through the approved pension scheme unless it is intended to provide an unapproved top-up pension. The pensions earnings cap makes this area particularly important.

¶704 Life assurance

Life assurance provides valuable security for employees, their family and dependants, and is relatively inexpensive to purchase. The provision of life assurance through a group arrangement works well in that not only can discounts be obtained, but also cover can be provided for relatively unhealthy employees who would not be able to obtain life cover on standard terms (and, indeed, may not be able to obtain life cover at all) on an individual basis.

While some group plans offer the benefit payable on death as a fixed monetary amount, most plans provide a benefit equal to a multiple of an employee's earnings, which may vary according to grade. Although there are tax advantages in providing the life assurance benefit through an exempt approved pension scheme, this effectively imposes a limit of four times earnings on the amount of lump sum benefit to be provided. There is also a limit on the maximum earnings than can be counted for this purpose, and the comments made in ¶703(5) apply here too.

(1) Including life assurance in flex plans

A life assurance benefit can normally be incorporated into a flexible benefits plan fairly easily. Typically, employees may opt for life assurance equal to a multiple of their earnings, with that multiple being chosen to suit their individual needs. However, many companies are reluctant to allow employees to take no cover at all. This reflects the position that the company may find itself in if faced with a widowed spouse with young children following the death of an employee who had opted out of the company's group life assurance arrangements, especially if the employee had chosen the options without discussing the matter with his or her spouse.

Whilst recognising this dilemma, it should be noted that there will be employees, in particular young employees with no dependants, who have no requirement for a life assurance benefit. It may be considered inappropriate to force such employees to opt for any life cover at all. A safeguard which can be incorporated to avoid at least some of the difficulties mentioned above is to require employees' spouses to sign election forms to indicate their consent to the level of cover chosen.

(2) Insurance issues

Most companies purchase life cover through an external insurer. This insurer may well be concerned if free choice is given to increase life cover when health or life expectancy is poor. This concern may be reflected in increased premiums and/or restrictive requirements for health examinations.

These can be avoided or reduced by discussing the proposed plan with insurers early on and agreeing an approach which might include one or more of the following:

- only allowing an increase in cover of one times salary at any election;
- requiring cover to remain constant for a period of two or, perhaps, three years;
- a minimum cover of two times salary.

¶705 Medical insurance

There has been a dramatic increase in the take-up of medical insurance both by individuals and companies on behalf of their employees. This has occurred despite the cost of providing medical insurance increasing significantly in recent years well in excess of the general rate of price inflation. This trend is likely to continue as a result of increased usage by members, and the introduction of highly sophisticated and expensive procedures for diagnosis and treatment of illness. Many companies are becoming concerned about the continued provision of private medical insurance in the light of these expected increases.

(1) Including medical insurance in flex plans

One of the advantages of incorporating private medical insurance in a flexible benefits plan is that the company can make visible, or pass on to staff, any future increases in the cost of providing the benefits. With the latter approach, employees will be faced with using more of their benefits credits in future simply to maintain the level of their benefits. If the overall credits remain fixed, benefits will have to be cut back in other areas.

A further advantage is that it may allow companies an opportunity to remove some of the anomalies and cross-subsidies that exist in providing company-paid private medical insurance, between the four main classes of membership (single member, member and spouse, member and family, and single parent).

If the company is currently committed to the cost of providing cover for eligible employees at the level each employee requires, single employees will effectively be subsidising married employees with families. Indeed, these cross-subsidies may be more acute since the benefit will be of no value to some employees, in particular, those who are covered for private medical insurance under their spouse's plan.

The consequence of eliminating these cross-subsidies is that credit will probably need to be given for full family cover if this is the entitlement. Additional costs will be incurred when employees who take cover only for themselves may be able to cash in on the difference between family cover credit and the price of single cover. This, if necessary, can be eliminated by adjusting credit allowances to provide for family cover *only if* this is taken.

Medical insurance is sometimes just as much a benefit to the employer as it is to the employee in that it can be used to bring the employee back to work quickly and efficiently after illness, and with minimum stress. Many employers would not wish to allow employees to opt out altogether unless perhaps there is continuing evidence that the employee is sufficiently covered in a plan operated by the spouse's employer.

(2) Structuring options

There are several different dimensions which can be flexed:

- number of people covered such as family, married and single persons cover;

¶705

- accommodation band, for example, BUPA bands A, B, or C;
- deductibles, such as the first £100 to be paid by the employee on any claim;
- scope of coverage, for example, comprehensive at one extreme or 'excessive waiting list only' at the other.

Options can be based on more than one of these factors, a common combination being the first two. The third option could be a valuable step in improving cost control as there is an incentive for employees to keep the number of claims to a minimum. On these grounds, this option could be priced attractively to encourage take up.

(3) Insurance issues

Medical insurers are usually more accustomed to employee choice than their group life assurance counterparts. There are also control mechanisms which exclude certain medical conditions if the employee was suffering at the time cover was taken up. For these reasons discussions with medical insurers should be less problematic although, again, these should be started early so that any restrictions which will avoid increases in premiums can be considered. As most large medical schemes work on a claims-related basis, any protection an insurer would want are also likely to be sensible for the company.

¶706 Long-term disability insurance

In many companies, the provision of long-term disability benefits (also known as permanent health insurance or sickness benefit) is considered not to be so much an employee benefit as a safety net for employees who are unable to perform their normal duties due to long-term illness. It should be borne in mind that, at most age groups, there is a greater likelihood of an employee becoming long-term disabled than dying. Thus insurers tend to be cautious on terms where employees have a choice of cover.

(1) Including disability benefits in flex plans

Some companies consider it inappropriate to flex disability benefit, particularly if it is not highly valued with a consequently low take-up rate. If it is flexed, most companies wish to impose a minimum level of cover for all employees.

The extent to which flexibility for disability benefits can be included is likely to be subject to two limiting factors: a maximum amount above which a company will not be able to insure the benefit, and a minimum below which an employer may be faced with difficulties in dealing with personnel issues relating to employees on long-term sick leave.

Generally, insurance companies are unwilling to provide sickness cover which results in total benefits (that is, benefits payable under the insurance contract and from the state) exceeding 75 per cent of an employee's income. This limit is not to be interpreted strictly since employees on low pay will receive certain flat-rate benefits from the state which often result in sickness benefits greater than 75 per cent of their income. Nevertheless, insurance companies would expect claims experience to deteriorate rapidly if benefits were generally provided in excess of 75 per cent of earnings prior to sickness. Not many employers would be willing to self-insure the excess risk since they would undoubtedly be faced with the same problems of high claim rates.

(2) Structuring options
There are two different dimensions which can be flexed:

- a choice in the level of cover could be, for example, 50 per cent or 75 per cent of salary;
- a choice in the rate of increase in payments could be, for example, zero or increasing at 5 per cent per annum.

(3) Insurance issues
The issues relating to insurance are very similar to those encountered with life assurance cover, although, as noted above, insurers may be more cautious.

¶707 Including holiday entitlement in flex plans

Flexing and pricing annual leave is relatively straightforward. However, there are a number of important personnel management issues to consider before introducing flexibility in this area.

In most cases, it is appropriate for employees to take a minimum amount of annual leave – if they do not there may be adverse implications for the employees' health and job performance. Similarly, it may not be possible for an employee to discharge his or her job responsibilities if an excessive number of days' holiday are taken. In practice, it should be feasible to flex holiday entitlement, but this is likely to be restricted to a fairly narrow range of annual leave such as between 20 and 30 days. In any case, restrictions on the number of consecutive days leave taken will be needed, as is the case outside a flex plan.

Cost increases can be experienced if those who have never taken their full entitlement are now allowed to cash in on the difference between take-up and entitlement. These can be limited by requiring selections to be made at the beginning of the year, disallowing any further adjustments to reflect actual take up.

¶708 Other benefits

In addition to the major benefits described above, there are others which commonly feature in flex plans. We comment briefly on each of these in turn.

(1) Professional advice for employees
Independent financial and tax advice will be appropriate for some employees, especially those in a flex plan, and a number of companies are taking the opportunity to make such advice available on a group basis. The benefit will not have universal appeal, but will be attractive to employees with a significant benefits package. Our experience shows that employees, even at executive level, are often not in a position to make fully informed decisions about the choices facing them.

The main difficulty in providing this benefit is that individual circumstances vary to such a great extent. Employees at the same grade may have significantly different personal and financial situations and this makes it very difficult to offer the benefit of employee advice on a standard basis. If the benefit is to be incorporated within a flexible benefits plan, it is likely that it will be provided at varying levels with the option to take no advice.

(2) Child care
Child care vouchers and crèche facilities are becoming increasingly attractive to both female and male employees, and to employers, as a way of retaining female staff in the workforce after maternity leave, or to encourage them to return after raising the family. A number of child care voucher systems have been developed which are available for spending by employees on approved child care facilities. The vouchers are relatively straightforward to administer. Alternatively, some employers may consider it appropriate to establish crèche facilities at work. This is really only practical for large employers at the moment but is likely to be perceived as a very attractive benefit, for returning mothers or single parents in particular, and will probably be welcomed by all employees in a flex plan.

(3) Education assistance
Increasingly, more parents wish to provide private education for their children. However, in difficult financial times, the expense of private education can be a strain on an employee's financial resources. The ability to opt for the benefit of education assistance in return for a reduction in other benefits is likely to be perceived as a major attraction for a certain category of employee. The employee needs to be aware of the implications of taking this benefit in lieu of a tax-free benefit.

(4) Dental/optical insurance
With increased health awareness, the demands currently being placed on the NHS and the cost of treatment, a number of employers are offering dental and optical insurance for employees. Such schemes can be easily included in a flexible benefits plan.

¶708

(5) Fitness facilities

Sport and fitness facilities are becoming increasingly popular for today's health conscious employees. This is a very straightforward benefit to administer and in certain circumstances it is a tax-free benefit.

(6) Car parking

Car parking can be both difficult and expensive, particularly in large city centres. Once again, the provision of a car parking benefit is simple to administer, is likely to be appreciated by a significant number of employees, and, within certain limits, it is a tax-free benefit.

8 Pricing The New Benefits Package – Issues

Executive summary
- Based on the design parameters, the next step is to price each benefit, the third step in the design loop (Figure 2).
- The true cost of each benefit will have an effect on price and will be a function of one or more of salary, age, and grade.
- It is important to determine a pricing philosophy which will establish whether employees will be in a position to buy back their existing benefits, if they choose, or whether the removal of cross-subsidies between benefits may make the existing benefits more expensive for certain groups.

¶801 Pricing an unknown quantity

Most organisations considering introducing a flexible benefits plan are nervous about pricing the new plan, and quite rightly so. Pricing such a plan requires actuarial analysis, particularly in respect of risk benefits, to set a price for each benefit. In determining the price for a benefit to be offered, there is a choice between the amount which represents the cost to the employer and the value to the employee. There are a number of factors causing these two amounts to be different, in particular:

- the purchasing power of the employer;
- more favourable terms associated with group arrangements;
- tax savings;
- National Insurance savings.

The eventual cost to the company of the benefit, however, will depend on:

- the take up of each benefit;
- the age and sex profile of employees who do take up the benefit.

The system of 'price tags' attached to each option must therefore be carefully worked out in order to ensure costs are controlled and the plan appears fair to employees.

The financial effect of the plan on both the employer and the employee is determined by the combination of the pricing system and the credit allowance which sets how much an individual can spend on his or her benefits. The detail of credit setting is covered in the next chapter, but the principles are touched upon here as pricing and credit setting are interdependent. Because of this, readers are advised to read both Chapters 9 and 10 before developing an approach on pricing. In any case, most readers are likely to need expert help in these areas.

¶802 Pricing philosophy – an overview

Before launching into a numerical analysis of costs and prices it is important to establish a philosophy or set of principles which will be used in setting the pricing system. Again, the objectives need to guide the approach.

It is important to understand the 'true cost' of each benefit, by which we mean the cost after eliminating all cross-subsidies between individuals with different characteristics. The true cost of each benefit is likely to be a function of one or more of the following factors:

- *Salary*: an example of a salary-related benefit is holiday entitlement since, although the benefit or entitlement may be linked to status or service, the cost to the employer of providing the benefit is influenced primarily by the individual's earnings. An obvious estimate of the cost would be annual earnings divided by the number of working days in a year *less* holiday allowance. A more sophisticated approach might be based upon the cost to the company of losing a day's work from that individual or indeed replacing the individual for the period of absence.
- *Age*: the cost of providing life assurance cover, for example, is dependent upon age. Indeed, for most companies it is also a function of salary and so the actual cost will be related to both an employee's age and his or her salary.
- *Grade*: the model or cost of company cars typically vary by grade of staff. For example, directors may be entitled to expensive executive cars whereas managers may only qualify for standard models. As directors are likely on the whole to be better paid, a correlation exists between the cost of the car and the individual's salary.
- *Fixed element*: some benefits cost the same for all employees irrespective of their grade, age or income. For example, providing dental treatment could be considered a fixed cost element within the benefits package.

Once the true costs have been established for the various benefits at their different levels, consideration can be given to weighting these if the employer wants to encourage or discourage take up of a particular benefit. For example, if a day's holiday entitlement costs £100 then setting the cost for an additional day's leave at £150 would clearly discourage an employee from taking up this option.

¶803 Pricing principles

There are five main philosophies or principles which can be adopted in developing a pricing system, some of which are in direct conflict:

- to ensure all employees can buy back their existing benefits;
- to use and be able to communicate the true cost;
- to avoid penalising older staff by charging higher prices;
- to award credits as a standard formula, probably based on salary;
- to maintain cost levels.

¶804 Pricing philosophy – a dilemma

Resolving the conflicts between these principles is probably the most challenging part of developing a flex plan.

For example, given that several of the main benefits such as disability, medical and life insurance and pension have aged-related dimensions, using the true cost implies incorporating an age-related scale in the pricing system. This would, however, be in conflict with an objective not to penalise older staff, but it would also mean that it would not be possible either to set a standard formula based on salary, or for all employees to be able to buy back their existing benefits. This is because a group of individuals of different ages will need different amounts to 'buy back' their existing packages through the plan, and this implies that credits cannot be allocated through a standard formula.

What about the alternative approach of ignoring age-related elements in benefit costs? This is certainly simpler and has the advantage of satisfying the first and fourth principles. However, this approach raises a potentially greater problem which is illustrated in Figure 10.

If an average cost is used as the option price, employees in the younger age group will tend to opt out of the benefit either because of the high price being charged, or because they have little perceived need for benefit. This will mean that those who are normally cross-subsidising the older group will no longer be included in this option. The overall cost to the company will increase as those who opt out would normally be awarded the equivalent of the price to use on other benefits or as an addition to salary. This is illustrated by the dotted line on the diagram.

This is an example of selection against the company, or adverse selection, terms which are frequently used in discussions about flexible benefits. It can apply in any of pension, life assurance, disability insurance and medical cover benefits.

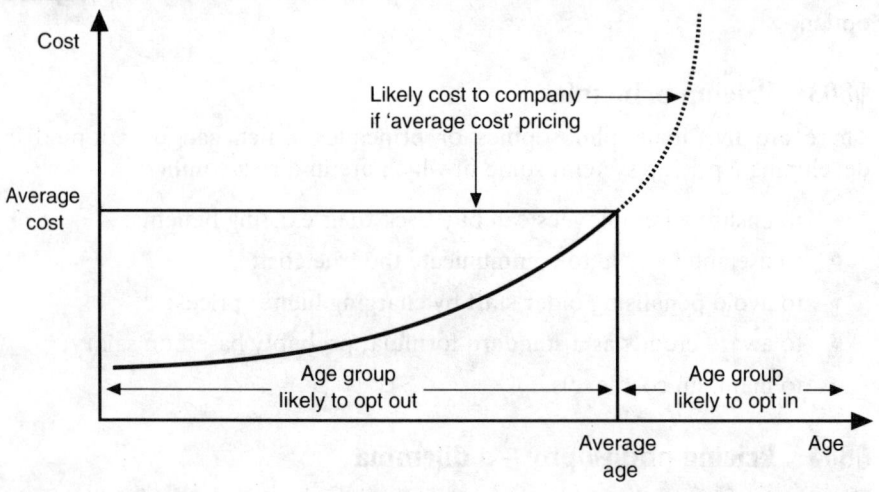

Figure 10: Effect of averaging the true cost of age-related benefits

To summarise, the effects of attempting not to penalise older staff can upset the general financial stability of the plan and means that there is an increase in costs. Clearly, also, as neither employees nor management would know the differences in cost which arise between individuals, the plan would fail to meet the principle of using and communicating true cost.

¶805 Pricing philosophy – a pragmatic approach

There is no perfect solution to this problem but the key is not to be defeated by the difficulties and, instead, to find a practical solution which meets the main objectives of the plan without being either over-complex or over-costly. This is possible with a pragmatic approach which may well differentiate between benefits in the particular treatment adopted.

For example, it may be judged that life assurance is so cheap a benefit that a fixed price can be charged irrespective of age. This price can be lifted above the current average without making the benefit prohibitively expensive for staff and the company may be willing to accept the risk of increases overall arising from individual choices.

¶806 Setting the prices

Having decided on a philosophy it is then necessary to calculate the prices to be used. This is a somewhat iterative process, partly because the actual level of prices may result in a revisit of the philosophy chosen and partly because the later stages of setting credits and costing the plan may well result in adjustments to the pricing system to be used.

¶807   The effects of selection

In implementing a flexible benefits plan, employers should:

- seek to identify those benefits where there is potential for adverse selection;
- evaluate the extent of the selection problem;
- model various take-up rates to predict the likely financial effect of selection;
- undertake some employee research to gain an indication of the likely take-up rate of the various benefits;
- impose some restrictions on the extent of the choice of certain benefits to offset the effects of adverse selection.

¶808   Company car

The pricing of a company car benefit involves a few complex issues. As mentioned in Chapter 7, each possible model can be separately priced or available models can be grouped into bands based on a particular benchmark or maximum cost. Either way, each model needs to be costed carefully to include all the different elements. The way in which company cars are treated regarding corporation tax, for example, may need to be allowed for when costing the benefit.

(1)   Cars – pricing a lease

A leased car scheme is more straightforward to incorporate into a flexible benefits plan than an outright purchase scheme, since a logical starting point for establishing the cost of providing the benefit would be annual lease cost plus an allowance for insurance costs. However, an adjustment may be necessary since lease costs are typically expressed as a level cost over a fixed period, say three or four years and for a fixed mileage but, typically, excluding insurance and fuel. This may not sit very comfortably within a plan which allows annual choice and involves updating the prices and allowances each year.

In these circumstances someone choosing not to take a car will normally gain an extra cash amount. This will possibly increase each year in line with salary, whereas previously the cost of the benefit would have remained constant for the period of the lease. In order to balance the costs of these two options more evenly and to avoid cost increases, the cash amount (and thus the price of the option it buys) may need to be reduced at the beginning of the lease period so that, by increasing each year over the period, it will equate to the lease cost.

¶808

(2) Cars – pricing the purchase of a car

If a company purchases its fleet of cars outright then it will need to convert the purchase price into an annual amount to price the benefit to employees, taking account of:

- depreciation,
- interest,
- servicing costs,
- insurance,
- road tax, and
- fuel, if provided as a benefit.

A quotation from a leasing company for the contract hire of a comparable car may be a good basis for costing depreciation, interest, servicing costs and road tax.

¶809 Risk benefits

Assuming a decision has been taken to allow for age-related differences in prices where appropriate, a matrix can be developed along the lines of Figure 11.

Actuarial expertise is needed in developing the entries in this matrix, and this is beyond the scope of this book. They will normally be derived from spreading the current average cost of each benefit over the existing employees covered in order to arrive at an age-related structure, and then developing a full table to cover all of the possible ages. In practice, it will often be sensible to group ages into bands of, say, five years.

¶810 Holiday entitlement

The pricing of annual holiday benefit can be based on a simple cost-of-a-day's-salary approach. Alternatively, the employer may wish to charge the cost of replacing the individual with temporary staff, or even the cost of lost production.

These costs may be additionally loaded to discourage excessive leave, although, at the other end of the scale, the employer will want to ensure that a minimum period of leave is taken each year. Finally, the extent to which unused holidays can be carried forward to the next year will need to be decided.

¶811 Other benefits

We have concentrated mainly on the so-called risk benefits as these present the greatest challenges in pricing terms. Many of the other benefits such as child care vouchers, financial advice, sports clubs – in short any benefit which

Benefit:	Life assurance			Disability insurance				Medical			
Unit:	% of salary			% of salary				£			
Benefit option (1):	2 × salary	3 × salary	4 × salary	⅓ salary		⅔ salary		Family		Single	
Benefit option (2):				Flat	5% increase	Flat	5% increase	Band A	Band B	Band A	Band B
Age:											
20											
21											
22											
23											
24											
25											
26											
27											
28											
29											
30											
31											
⋮											
58											
59											
60											

Figure 11: Matrix of costs allocated on an age-related basis

¶811

involves the company in a simple annual (or more frequent) cash payment – are very simple to cost. This will normally be priced using that payment, allowing for VAT if appropriate. Departures can clearly be made if the company wishes to subsidise a particular benefit for example, to pay for the administration charges on child care vouchers.

The pricing of benefits such as share options is complex, and beyond the scope of this book.

9 Setting Credit Allowances

Executive summary
- To complete the pricing exercise, the third step in the design loop shown in Figure 2, you need also to set the credit allowance, or how much each employee will have available to spend. Especially if the credits are weighted to encourage or discourage take-up, the overall pricing exercise will have a major impact on the cost to the employer at the next stage.
- The employer must decide at this stage whether or not it will allow some employees to gain, or others to lose out as a result of the new benefits package.
- There are two principal methods used to derive credit allocations: a formula, often a percentage of salary, or a tabular approach based on statistical techniques.

¶901 Introduction
The final critical piece in the flex plan design jigsaw is the setting of credit allowances. Along with the pricing system used, these determine the cost of the plan to the company and the way in which credit allowances are set and could have a fundamental impact on the way in which the whole benefits package is viewed in the future.

As emphasised earlier, this part of plan design is iterative and complex and it is important to read the next chapter on plan costing before developing an approach to the setting of plan credits.

¶902 What are credits?
Credits are the notional allocation given to employees to 'buy' the benefits of their choice. The advantages and disadvantages of using money or points was discussed in ¶607.

¶903 How are the credits set?
In order to increase acceptance of the plan it will normally be necessary to ensure that each employee is able, with the allocated credits, to buy back at least his or her existing level of benefit. If this were the sole objective of the

credits policy, the simplest way of achieving this would be to grant credits at a level so that every employee gains exactly the credit equivalent of their existing benefits – they simply gain the flexibility to spend these credits as they wish.

Some flex plans in the US work on the basis of separate credits for each benefit rather than one overall allowance. This is useful in dealing with issues or constraints connected with one particular benefit, but the advantage of having a global benefit cost figure is lost.

¶904 Winners and losers

There are some circumstances in which it will not be possible to use a formula-driven approach, and to understand this it is important also to understand the concept of 'winners and losers' as it can upset the best formulated plan.

The idea of winners and losers comes from considering how an individual could replicate his or her existing package through the plan. Even if few staff would want to do this, most employees would want to test the plan on this basis in any case. Employees are winners if they obtain an excess credit allowance through having selected their existing package. They are losers if they have to give up salary in order to recreate their existing benefits package.

Managing the winners and losers effectively will be critical both to the acceptance of the plan by employees and to the cost of the plan to the company.

Winners and losers will be limited if credit allowances and prices are set so that the credits are very close to the total of the prices of existing benefits for each eligible employee. If they are not close, protection may need to be given to the losers in order to pull them into the plan but it is normally difficult to recoup this from the winners. This will clearly result in additional costs.

¶905 Two methods to derive credit allocations

There are two principal methods used to derive credit allocations:

- a formula-driven approach;
- a tabular approach.

Most companies would like to achieve a simple formula so that they will know that, for example, 'the benefits package will always cost us 25 per cent of salary'. This relates back to the pricing objectives discussed in Chapter 8.

To decide which approach is appropriate it is advisable to examine any underlying patterns that may exist in the benefit structure. The example in Figure 12 illustrates these points.

¶904

> An employer limits its company cars so that the annual lease charge must not exceed 15% of salary with the salary for this purpose limited to £50,000.
>
> For earners below £50,000 the maximum annual value of the car is therefore a simple proportion of salary.
>
> For earners above £50,000 the maximum car value is a fixed amount.
>
> It is sensible therefore to split the plan into two (salary above and below £50,000 respectively) and to use the underlying formula explicitly in deriving the credit allocation. So that the credit allocation can be broken down as:
>
> - 15% of salary for people below £50,000; and
> - fixed at £7,500 (15% of 50,000) for those earning above £50,000.

Figure 12: Establishing a formula for credit allocations

¶906 A formula-driven approach

With a formula-driven approach, a simple formula is calculated to derive and explain credit allocations. There are a number of ways of doing this, all of which aim to find a formula which shows the cost of all of the underlying benefits as a function of salary, for example, say, credits will be 10 per cent of salary plus £150.

(1) Which benefits should be included in a formula-driven approach?

In principle, the credit allocation will cover those elements of the existing package which are allocated a price tag. This will normally relate to the entitlement in each benefit, rather than the actual take up. There are three possible approaches:

- price all benefits (including any which are required as part of the core). In these circumstances the credit allowance roughly represents the cost of all benefits which the company has previously provided;
- price all core benefits at zero and base the credit formula on the excess package over and above the core;
- price the current package at zero and express options up from this level as deductions from salary (or other benefits) and options down as additions to salary (or other benefits). An advantage is that it focuses on something which is known to employees, their existing package. However, a disadvantage of this approach is that it fails to communicate a clear message of value.

(2) How is a formula set?

There are three main approaches:

- Some benefits such as pension contributions and annual leave are formula-driven. If several benefits can be identified in this way then a formula which is the total of all the underlying formulae may be appropriate.

- A 'median person' approach where, for a group, the employer identifies a hypothetical median person with regard to his or her age, sex, salary, etc. The employer identifies the average benefit entitlements and the cost of these is expressed as a percentage of the median salary. Although this is more likely to be used for plans with a large coverage, the example in Figure 13 for a plan for ten employees illustrates how the method works.

Initials	Sex	Age	Salary £	Life assurance cost (3 × salary) £	Car lease cost (annual) £	PMI cover £
AB	M	30	20,000	90	3,000	250
AC	M	25	18,000	45	3,000	300
AD	M	32	20,000	92	3,000	350
AE	F	35	30,000	120	3,500	350
AF	M	38	35,000	180	3,800	350
AG	M	40	40,000	250	5,000	350
AH	M	35	32,000	150	3,800	300
AI	M	31	30,000	140	3,800	300
AJ	M	28	25,000	110	3,000	350
AK	F	30	20,000	75	3,000	300

Description of median person
Average age: 32.4
Sex: male
Salary: £27,000

Average benefit costs
Life assurance: £125.20
Car lease cost: £3,200.00
PMI cover: £320.00
Total: £3,945.20

As a percentage of average salary: 15%

Figure 13: Example scheme: membership details and true benefit costs

¶906

- Another approach is to fit a line (or perhaps a curve) to the total benefit values of all staff concerned using regression techniques. This can be done automatically using a spreadsheet. The first step is to plot the cost of the current benefits on a graph against salary (Figure 14) and then to plot a line through these. A straight-line approach is often chosen for simplicity, but the aim is to get the best possible fit to the points plotted.

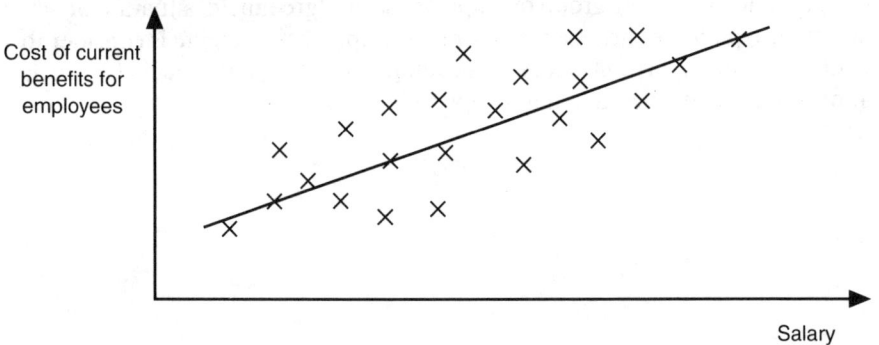

Figure 14: The cost of current benefits

Having derived the formula, it is essential to establish the impact on the cost of the plan. The mechanics of this costing are covered in Chapter 10. However, it is possible to limit the effects of any cost increases by managing the effect of the particular formula in terms of the winners and losers it creates. This is done by ensuring the formula is as good a fit as possible to the total prices of the existing package for each person. This fit can be improved by splitting the eligible group into sub-groups which are perhaps more homogeneous in terms of age, salary and/or grade. See Chapter 10 for more on this.

It is normally feasible to derive a formula for credit allowances. But in some circumstances a good enough 'fit' to the existing package cannot be obtained and a tabular approach is necessary.

¶907 A tabular approach

A tabular approach involves deriving a table of individual credit values which will probably closely match the total prices of the existing benefits package for each individual. The disadvantage of this approach is that the concept of a uniform benefits package which is a predictable additional cost to salary is lost. The advantage is that winners and losers should not exist by definition.

If this approach is adopted, a gradual phasing into a credit formula is possible as salaries increase in future years. For example an individual's credit could be '25 per cent of salary or £5,000 if higher', the £5,000 being fixed as the individual credit needed at the outset to recreate the existing package.

¶907

¶908 Summing up

Pricing and setting credits are complex parts of the design of a flex plan. They are areas where most companies need expert advice and support – this is well worthwhile as the consequences of getting the structure wrong can range from a poorly understood plan to a catastrophically expensive one.

We have focused on coping with the constraints imposed by an existing package and an existing group of employees. In a 'greenfield' situation or when designing a plan (or part of a plan) for new employees only, life is considerably easier, and an opportunity exists to develop a simple benefits package which is at once well controlled and highly appreciated.

10 Costing the Plan

Executive summary

- To close the design loop, the final stage is costing the new plan. In practice, it will probably be necessary to work through Steps 2, 3 and 4 of the design loop shown in Figure 2 several times before you are satisfied with all the design elements and the impact on the cost to the employer.
- In particular, it may be necessary to re-work the plan because of the impact on winners and losers.
- To test how robust the plan is, the first step is to calculate the worst-case cost, and from there to test a number of 'what-if' scenarios.

¶1001 Introduction

It is clearly essential to know the cost of a plan before seeking final agreement to its introduction. As the costs are determined to a large extent by the pricing and credit system these may need to be adjusted once the plan is fully costed. However, the ultimate cost of the plan is determined by the choices employees make and the ultimate benefit costs based on actual (rather than assumed) experience in each benefit. At this stage, therefore, it is important to model the impact of different choices and experience on the plan to test its robustness.

¶1002 Developing a cost model

A database of all eligible employees needs to be set up in order to cost the plan accurately. This is usually done by means of a spreadsheet which although simple in concept, can become rather large, so it is worthwhile ensuring sufficient computer memory exists before starting. A framework for this costing model is shown in Figure 15.

This framework can be used to cost the new plan on the basis of existing benefits actually taken up. In this way it will identify winners and losers in the two columns headed 'gain' and 'loss', and shows the impact of the plan on the individual.

If the flex prices are a close estimate of the true cost of each benefit option then the framework will also show the cost to the employer of the plan (assuming existing benefits are taken up through the flex plan).

Flexible Benefits

Employee data					Car		Life assurance		Benefits: Medical			Money purchase pension		Total	Credit allowance £	Gain £	Loss £	Special allowance for losers £	Net loss position £
Name	Date of birth	Salary	Grade || Model	Flex price £	Multiple of salary	Flex price £	Cover	Band	Flex price £	Contribution rate	Flex price £	Flex price £					
1*	2	3	4 || 5	6	7	8	9	10	11	12	13	14	15	16	17	18	19

* = column number

Figure 15: A framework for costing

¶1002

However, if flex prices are not a close estimate of true cost (see Chapter 9), an extra column should be added for each benefit to show the true cost to the employer of providing the benefit. This should then be used instead of Column 14 in all calculations.

The cost of the plan is the sum:

Column 15 (credit allowance)

plus

Column 18 (special allowance for losers).

This can then be compared against the cost of the existing plan to work out the incremental cost or saving of the flex plan.

¶1003 Winners and losers

As has been emphasised earlier, the fact that there may be winners and losers can have a fundamental effect on the financial impact of the plan. This is confirmed by the formulae shown above in ¶906(2). The treatment of losers will also have a major impact on how well the plan is accepted by staff.

As stated earlier, it is important that the credit allowance provides a good fit against the total prices of existing benefits. It is at this stage that a bad fit will become apparent, as there will be a large number of people who win or lose by more than, say, 0·5 per cent of their salary. If the plan is introduced at the same time as a salary increase, this band of tolerance will probably be wider as employees can be encouraged to compare their total package before both flex and the salary increase, with the total package afterwards. If salaries are to increase by 5 per cent or more this gives a lot of scope for absorbing losers without a major problem. However, in current times salary increases are often minimal and, in any case, it may not be possible to combine the two.

(1) Limiting the effect of winners and losers

There are several possible ways of limiting the winners and losers including:

- if the credit formula is statistically set, eliminate extreme cases and refit;
- if a 'median person' approach has been taken, split the group into two or three sub-groups to produce a greater uniformity within each;
- if the formula has been based on underlying cost, carry out an analysis to determine the source of variability between individuals and model this element separately;
- Revisit the pricing structure to ensure a better fit.

(2) Protecting the losers

Having taken steps to minimise the winners and losers it may still be necessary to protect losers. There are several options here:

- increase the credit allocation globally to convert losers into winners. This is unlikely to be practical in a large scale plan as costs can be high;
- add an additional percentage of salary to the credit allowance for losers to bridge the gap;
- apply a fixed additional amount to bridge the gap (not to be increased in future years);
- apply a fixed additional amount and reduce and remove this once the standard credit formula exceeds the original credit in pounds;
- fix initial credits so that the credit is close to the total package price for both winners and losers gradually moving both onto a standard formula in time.
- do nothing, and allow the losers to remain on the current package.

(3) Limiting the impact of winners

There may also be scope for limiting the impact of winners where it is apparent that specific groups are consistent winners. A special case of winners occurs when staff do not currently take up all the benefits entitlement. Examples are:

- single people who do not take up married or family medical cover;
- car schemes where staff taking a cheaper car are not recompensed;
- mortgage schemes where many are not at the maximum benefit level.

Normally, a credit allowance would allow for the full entitlement or perhaps the average take up. If an individual continues with their existing benefit then the difference between the credit allowance and the flex price of their benefit will be a gain.

Measures can be taken to limit this effect:

- only offer the full allocation if the full 'standard' entitlement is taken up, for example, if full family medical cover is standard, credits for this are only available if it is currently taken up (this obviously means that an existing arbitrary inconsistency between employees will continue).
- where cars are concerned only give access to a car credit on renewal of the company car. This only delays the effect, but could be valuable. However, it does not eliminate the effect in relation to those who currently refuse a car altogether.

¶1004 Testing for robustness

The model developed above can also be used to test the impact of other selections on the plan both from the employee's and employer's viewpoints.

A worst-case scenario can be put into the model by using an algorithm which picks the selections for each person which turn out to be the worst for the company. This would only occur if prices are used which differ from the true cost.

If an *average-age* cost approach is used in any benefits, the model should assume that all people who are younger than average will opt out of the benefits so far as they are permitted, and all those who are older than average will opt for the highest level of benefit. A modification of this would assume that those who opt out could buy the benefit more cheaply themselves. If cars are banded with one benchmark the model should assume all selections are at the top of the band.

This analysis will give a worst case cost. It may be sensible to develop a series of intermediate cases which might be regarded as realistic as individuals are unlikely to behave in the way predicted by the worst case approach.

¶1005 Closing the loop

As has been mentioned several times, developing the financial structure of the plan may need to be repeated several times with minor alterations. It is critical that the plan's objectives are used as a guide at every stage. Inevitably, some of these objectives may need to be compromised or re-prioritised in order to allow the plan as a whole to work. It is important that, once the plan has been refined as far as it can be, the final design is tested to ensure that objectives and cost constraints have been met as far as possible.

11 Income Tax, National Insurance Contributions and VAT – in Relation to Flex

Executive summary

- Income tax, National Insurance contributions and VAT all affect the potential design of a flex plan because of the traps and liabilities they may cause.

- It is preferable to gain approval from the relevant authorities for the plan design before implementation.

¶1101 Taking taxes into account

Income tax, National Insurance contributions and VAT will play their part in the overall design of a flex plan, and there are some traps which, if they are not avoided, can create unexpected and unnecessary additional tax liabilities. In those circumstances, both employer's costs and employee motivation can be severely affected.

This chapter summarises the key issues which need to be taken into account in the design of a flex plan. These issues are discussed further in Appendix 2 for those who would like more details on these underlying factors. Each plan must be designed with these potential traps in mind, and you will need to take advice from your professional advisers before progressing too far with the overall design.

In practice, many companies will obtain Inland Revenue and Customs & Excise clearance for a plan before implementing their plan in order to be fully satisfied that there are no hidden traps left. It is best to liaise, through your professional advisers, with the authorities at an early stage in the design process so that the new plan has their support.

¶1102 Income tax

A major way in which a plan can be affected by income tax is the timing and frequency of the selection of benefits. Elections should be no more frequent than once a year to avoid the risk of the employee being taxed on the higher of any cash alternatives he or she could, but does not, receive, and the taxable value, if any, of the benefit he or she does receive.

There is a fine line between receiving salary with which the employee pays for benefits and receiving a salary together with an entitlement to benefits in kind. The distinction is however fundamental to avoiding unexpected tax liabilities.

Employees should make decisions about future earnings only and should not be able to alter their choices outside the agreed election period (except in special circumstances).

The employee's contractual entitlement should be to receive a fixed salary together with the benefits or additional cash which he or she chooses – although any formal service contract might refer to a base salary of a certain amount plus entitlement to participate in the employer's flexible benefits plan.

(1) Receiving a benefit in lieu of a bonus

An employee may be given the choice of receiving a bonus payment in cash or by way of a benefit. However this choice must be offered before the entitlement to the bonus has arisen. The employee will then be taxed on what he or she receives, be it cash or the taxable value of the benefit chosen. The valuation of benefits for tax purposes is a separate topic which is discussed in more detail in Appendix 2.

(2) Sacrificing a part of salary

If an employee is given the opportunity of taking a lower salary and benefit, or the base salary and no benefit, they may be taxed on the value of the higher salary and the value of the benefit taken. Examples are given in Appendix 2.

(3) Taking cash as an alternative

If cash is the only alternative to a benefit not chosen, or cash is taken as the balance of unutilised credits, the employee is taxed on the amount of cash received additional to that taken as a benefit.

¶1103 VAT

If employees are required to contribute towards the cost of a benefit provided to them, the contribution is consideration for VAT purposes, and VAT may be due.

If employees apply salary already earned to a benefit then not only are there income tax implications as described above, but the sum applied will also be consideration for VAT purposes, and VAT may be due. It is important therefore to structure the contract to avoid the application of salary earned.

¶1104 National Insurance contributions

Employers' and employees' National Insurance contributions are due on cash taken in lieu of benefits. They are not due on benefits in kind, except for cars and some special cases. It will, therefore, be expensive for an employer to pay cash in lieu of benefits unless account is taken of NIC costs in the formula. The point is discussed more fully in Appendix 2.

¶1105 Conclusion

Each of these taxation issues is complex and may affect the cost of the scheme for both the employee and employer. It is critical to ensure that these far-reaching implications are considered early on in the plan design.

12 Employment Law and Flexible Benefits

Executive summary

- Introducing a flexible benefits plan for existing employees will require a change to their contracts of employment.
- Employees need to agree to the changes in their benefit plan.
- It is essential that the design of the plan takes full account of legislative requirements in terms of equal pay and sex discrimination.
- Legal advice is essential to ensure that an otherwise excellent plan does not falter because of the complexity of employment law.

¶1201 A change in employment contracts

Introducing a flexible benefits plan will involve changing the contracts of employment for existing employees. As there is no 'Flexible Benefits Act' and no case law on flexible benefits, it is important to consider how these changes can be introduced without running the risk of legal action by employees. We also point out the risk that employers may inadvertently discriminate against female employees – or against male employees – when introducing changes to pay and other benefits. Employers should also bear in mind that introduction of a flexible benefits plan provides a good opportunity to remedy inadequacies which presently exist in pay or in the documentation of contracts with staff, and to remove any such inequalities.

Contracts of employment, like other contracts, are founded on agreement. An employer cannot unilaterally impose changes in terms and conditions without breaking the contract. If an employer does impose a unilateral reduction in benefits on employees, the employees are likely to pursue the following options:

- resign and claim they have been unfairly dismissed;
- apply for an injunction to restrain the employer;
- indicate that they do not accept the changes, continue working normally and subsequently sue for any financial loss.

¶1202 The need for employees' consent

Any amendment to the terms and conditions under which an employee is employed requires the employee's consent before it can be implemented. This applies to all terms and conditions, whether express or implied, written or established by conduct.

The most obvious way in which an employer can obtain consent is by asking employees specifically to agree to the changes. Some of the changes may involve reducing the amount of cash paid to individual employees. Such reductions may amount, in effect, to deductions from pay. If so, the Wages Act 1986 will make it unlawful to implement such changes unless the employee has specifically agreed in advance to them in writing.

However attractive the overall plan may be, employees may object to one or two of the changes which the employer proposes to implement and they are entitled to do this. It will, therefore, be important to obtain agreement to all the changes in one go. It is common to do this by associating the changes with the employees' annual pay award. Unless the changes are significantly to their detriment, employees are unlikely to want to refuse the plan.

¶1203 What if the employees do not want flexible benefits?

If the employees do refuse the plan, the only way in which the employer can proceed with the changes would be by dismissing the employees and offering them re-employment on new terms which implement the flexible benefits plan. The difficulty with this approach is that it opens the door to unfair dismissal claims by all employees who have been dismissed. Although it is possible – depending on the circumstances – that the employer could, if the matter went to tribunal, succeed in establishing that the dismissals were fair, the employer would still be put to the trouble and expense of defending the claim.

For these reasons it would seem to follow that the only realistic option is for the employer to introduce the changes as part of the annual salary review and for the package to be made sufficiently attractive to make virtually certain that the employees will accept it.

¶1204 Equal pay and sex discrimination

The area of sex discrimination and equal pay is increasingly important in employment law. Indeed, with the various EC directives on such matters as equal pay and equal treatment, it will continue to play an important part. Again, the individual circumstances of a flexible benefits programme will determine whether or not there are relevant considerations. There may be a real risk that by changing the rules under which employees become entitled to benefits, the employer may inadvertently discriminate either against men or women. For instance, there are fewer female employees over 30 than male employees in the employed population. By restricting the right to participate in the pension scheme to employees over 30, the employer could introduce a requirement which female employees would find it more difficult to meet.

Furthermore, a plan may discriminate indirectly against women if part-time employees are excluded. It is quite possible that this discrimination can be justified, but it is important to think through this justification in advance, to avoid being faced with a successful industrial tribunal claim. Maternity provision is another area in which it would be easy to discriminate inadvertently. Will the plan provide the same benefits to employees absent on maternity leave as it provides to employees absent for a similar period because of illness?

Similarly, restricting certain terms and conditions to new employees could introduce inequalities in the pay and benefits system which may enable members of one sex to make equal pay claims against members of the other.

Such claims will be brought under s.1(3) of the Equal Pay Act 1970. Under this Act, it is possible, on certain grounds, for an employer to justify differences in pay which are indirectly discriminatory. It is important, therefore, that the benefits plan is designed to have regard to these issues, and that the justification for any discriminatory consequences is carefully thought through before it is introduced.

Employers need to anticipate problems and draft the plan rules to take account of them. For instance, most leavers will go part-way through the year. If the plan is to provide benefits which last after termination of employment – annual club membership, for instance – the costing and design of the plan will need to make this clear.

¶1205 Summary checklist

Bearing these considerations in mind, it is recommended that the following steps are taken at the appropriate stages in the design and implementation of a flexible benefits plan:

- *Establish the terms of the contract of employment.* This will be fairly simple if the company is well organised and the terms of employment are contained in one document – for instance, a contract of employment or staff handbook. Even in such cases, care needs to be taken to ensure that individual's terms have not been subsequently varied by correspondence, practice or oral agreement. Care also needs to be taken to ensure that the terms cover all the employees who will be covered by the flexible benefits plan, especially the most senior and the most junior. In less well-organised companies the terms of employment may not be written down at all or they may be included in correspondence. For long-serving employees, the relevant correspondence may stretch back many years.

- *Establish the changes which must be made to introduce the flexible benefits plan.* It is possible that no changes in the contract will be needed, but, if fundamental terms are to be altered, care must be taken when introducing the plan. If a fundamental term of their contract is broken, employees will be entitled to resign and claim constructive dismissal.
- *How will the terms of employment introduced by the plan be recorded?* Will the terms of the flexible benefits plan be set out in a stand-alone document, be incorporated in a contract of employment or staff handbook, pension scheme or other documentation, or be recorded only in correspondence?
- *Check whether the plan will be discriminatory.* Will the changes made by the plan adversely affect an individual because of his or her sex or marital status?
- *Decide in what form the flexible benefits plan will be introduced – by agreement or by terminating employment and offering employment on new terms.* In most cases the plan will be introduced by agreement. It would only be appropriate to terminate employment and offer employment on new terms where one or two recalcitrant individuals refuse to agree to participate and it was not practical for the company to allow their employment to continue on the old terms.
- *Decide the timing for introduction of the flexible benefits plan.* Changes to contract terms are often introduced at the same time as the annual pay increase. This is an easier way of obtaining employees' agreement.
- *Draft any new terms.* Bear in mind that any new contractual terms will need to be incorporated into the contract of employment, and that they will need to be contractually enforceable. Remember also that any deductions from pay should be agreed in advance in writing to satisfy the Wages Act 1986.
- *Ensure that the employees covered by the plan actually sign.* The contracts will only be valid when the employees indicate their consent.

¶1206 Drafting the plan

A major part of the legal input will go into drafting the rules of the plan, which are an important part of the contract of employment. The plan must define the benefits in a way which is tax-efficient, and needs to be drafted to:

- incorporate other elements in the contract – for instance the staff handbook and the other terms of the original contract;
- clearly define the rights of the parties in a way which makes them enforceable;

- communicate the rules of the plan in a way which makes them easy to operate and eliminates potential for misunderstanding;
- authorise any deductions from salary.

¶1207　Introducing the plan

Finally, care will be needed in introducing the plan. There are at least two legal risks.

It is possible that by introducing the plan the employer may inadvertently break employees' contracts of employment so that employees can claim that they have been constructively dismissed. Provided the level of benefits is at least as great as that under the contract it replaces, good communication should be sufficient to persuade employees to agree (but correspondence needs to be vetted by a lawyer).

The other risk is that the documentation does not clearly establish that rights under the original contract of employment are extinguished. If this is not dealt with properly it may be possible for:

- the Inland Revenue to seek income tax on the previous level of pay;
- employees to claim in months or years to come that they are entitled to arrears of salary or compensation for lost benefits.

Although an employer could reasonably conclude that only a very ungrateful employee would make such a claim, it would be embarrassing to have to concede to an employee who has been dismissed that he or she had indeed been underpaid.

13 Flexible Benefits for International Managers and Overseas Assignments

Executive summary
- Two key aspects that need to be addressed on international assignment policy are those of:
  - cost control,
  - motivation.
- Since these are the key benefits of a flex policy, there must be an argument for introducing flex into international assignments.
- We think that most organisations will implement flex in the various countries that they operate in first, and this will then act as a driver to its being incorporated into the international assignment policy.

¶1301 Cost control issues

With increasing emphasis on cost control, many employers have recognised the significant cost of overseas assignments. In many cases where costs were borne by both the domestic employer and the overseas host, the true costs were and remain unknown.

Many assignment packages have been individually designed, and set a precedent for future secondees, with inevitably escalating cost.

Tax has a significant impact on cost. In certain circumstances, tax in some countries can be avoided completely, but, if the employee stays one day too long, a whole year's earnings can become taxable. Some benefits are taxable in some countries, but not in others. Some employees may be taxable in two countries with differing tax rates, different methods of valuing benefits, different tax exemptions, or even tax years.

These issues can be overcome by a tax equalisation policy by which the employer bears the burden of additional taxes. The purpose of tax equalisation is to ensure that an expatriate does not take home less or more basic salary on assignment than he or she would otherwise have taken home.

As a result of tax equalisation, however, the employer may pay twice for benefits granted to an expatriate – once for the benefit itself, and then again for the tax on the benefit. Furthermore, most tax equalisation policies give expatriates no incentive to minimise tax costs.

¶1302 Motivational issues

It is well known that employers are finding it increasingly difficult to attract individuals into taking overseas assignments; particularly where dual income families are involved. International remuneration policies have to cater for a greater variety of needs than domestic policies and it is very difficult to set a standard package. An employee's requirements would be very different in Manhattan, a new development in the desert, or in eastern Europe, before any of his or her individual circumstances are taken into account. Furthermore, most people do not fit in to the category of 'most people'. The traditional stereotype of an expatriate no longer exists, yet there are a number of traditionally established policies created for them!

¶1303 The current situation

Most international assignment policies are costly and fail to make use of the opportunity to enhance motivation and to entice more managers into going overseas.

¶1304 How flex might be introduced

An effective international assignment policy for professionals requires a single reward policy, unaffected as far as possible by the peculiarities of employment and reward policies in the countries in which managers are resident for a period.

If the pay and benefits policy is set on a country by country basis many constraints must be taken into account, not the least in respect of pensions. In addition, each country has its own approach to benefits such as the number of days' holiday, company cars and health insurance. If an employer introduces a flexible benefits approach for its international managers, it can set one policy, and each manager can select from the same range of benefits those most appropriate to his or her circumstances and the country in which he or she is working. The overall cost can also be contained by including tax equalisation as a flexible benefit.

In this way a flexible benefits plan can offer choices that reflect the differing lifestyles of the managers as well as the differing cultures of the countries where they are assigned. The cost of the policy can be preset so that the employer has a finite liability for all benefits, including that of tax equalisation.

¶1304

14 Administration

Executive summary

- The best system to administer a flexible benefits plan will depend on the complexity of the plan, the number of employees in the plan, the IT infrastructure and some practical considerations.
- The four main options are a manual system, a spreadsheet or database, an integrated payroll and personnel system, or a dedicated flex system.
- The system must be able to fulfil four main functions – selection of benefits by employees, ongoing administration, financial reporting and cost control, and statutory reporting.
- It is critical to consider the links with other systems used by the organisation.
- The appropriate system needs to be supported by the right people, procedures and documentation.

¶1401 Introduction

Flexible benefits plans involve an additional layer of administration on top of existing benefit plans. However, companies with experience of running flexible benefit plans have found that this additional workload is nothing like the nightmare of popular belief provided the right approach is taken at the outset. Assuming the administration is to be done in-house, it is essential to:

- choose the right type of system for the plan and organisation;
- ensure links with other systems are established;
- train selected staff;
- develop sound and efficient procedures and documentation.

An alternative and often simpler solution is to contract out the administration to a specialist third party.

This chapter looks at the options available and gives guidance on developing the right solution for your organisation.

¶1402 The nature of the system

The best system for administering flexible benefits will depend on the nature of the organisation. A number of factors will impact on the choice:

- The complexity of the plan:
    (a) number and type of benefits included;
    (b) frequency of choices;
    (c) extent of flexibility in each benefit;
    (d) complexity of the pricing and credits system.
- The size of the organisation/plan:
    (a) numbers of employees included;
    (b) location and distribution of staff (number of sites, etc.);
    (c) resources available to administer the plan.
- IT infrastructure:
    (a) in-house IT support availability;
    (b) IT awareness and skill levels among staff;
    (c) complexity/sufficiency of existing systems;
    (d) need for links to other systems (e.g. payroll);
    (e) plans for future systems development.
- Practical considerations:
    (a) capital and maintenance costs;
    (b) available space;
    (c) existing equipment (terminals, wiring, etc.).

¶1403 Choosing a solution – the options

Figure 16 sets out the four main options to be considered when choosing a system to administer flexible benefits, with a brief discussion of benefits and disadvantages. Figure 17 summarises the suitability of these different options to schemes of varying complexity, from the simplest to the most sophisticated.

Solution	Benefits	Disadvantages
Manual system	• Low cost for scheme with small numbers	• Time consuming • Limited analysis and reporting • No automatic links to other systems

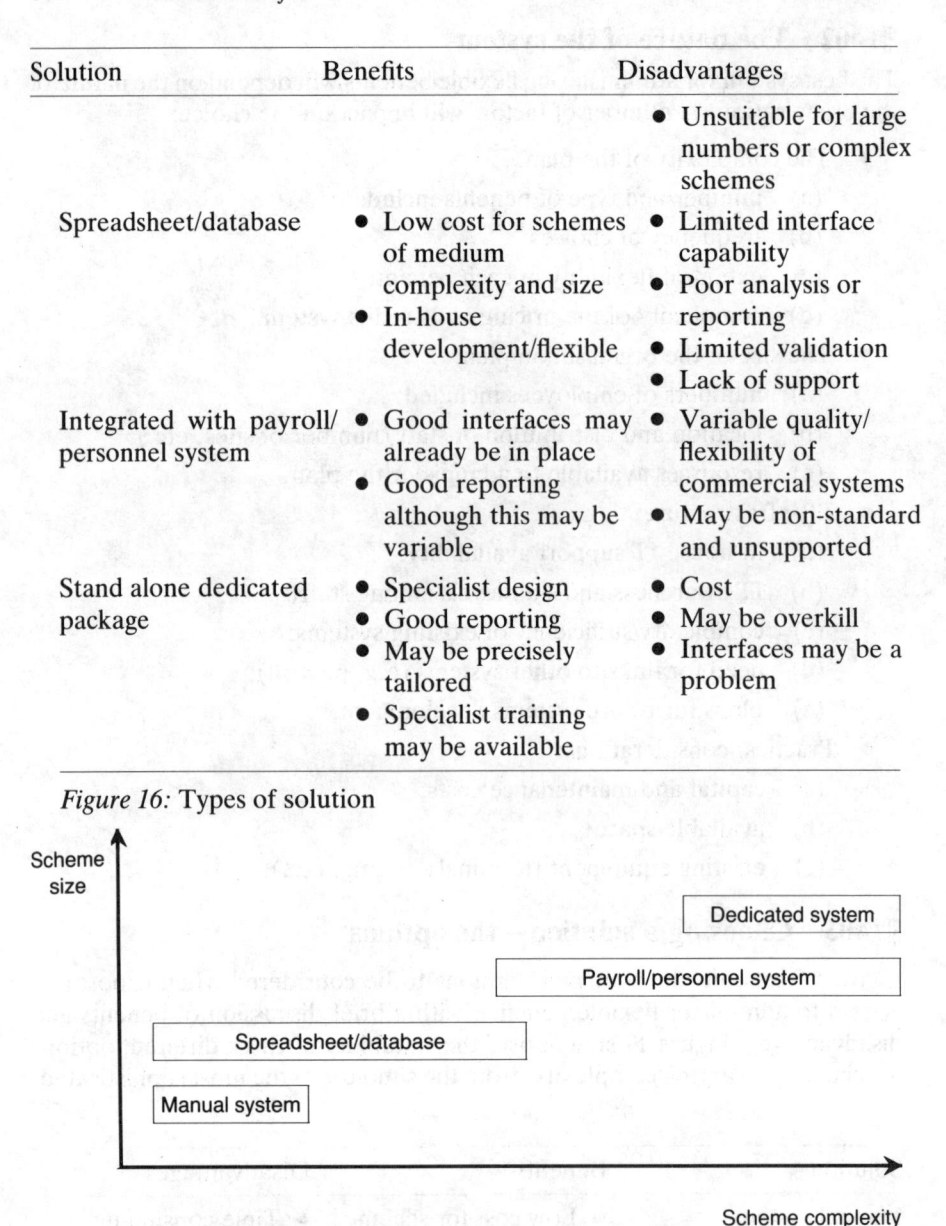

Solution	Benefits	Disadvantages
Spreadsheet/database	• Low cost for schemes of medium complexity and size • In-house development/flexible	• Unsuitable for large numbers or complex schemes • Limited interface capability • Poor analysis or reporting • Limited validation • Lack of support
Integrated with payroll/personnel system	• Good interfaces may already be in place • Good reporting although this may be variable	• Variable quality/flexibility of commercial systems • May be non-standard and unsupported
Stand alone dedicated package	• Specialist design • Good reporting • May be precisely tailored • Specialist training may be available	• Cost • May be overkill • Interfaces may be a problem

Figure 16: Types of solution

Figure 17: Which systems solution?

¶1404 Selecting a system – key functions

Any flexible benefits system must be able to fulfil four key functions:

¶1404

- selection of benefits by employees;
- ongoing administration;
- financial reporting and cost control;
- statutory reporting.

The main focus of attention for administration is often the first two functions listed, but the reporting features are also essential for internal and external control of the system. In a large organisation these are most usefully incorporated within a computerised system.

The table in Figure 18 can be used as a checklist to ensure that systems under consideration can fulfil all four key functions, during input, processing and output. Required features are listed for all key functions, at each stage in the system.

	Selection of benefits	Ongoing administration	Financial reporting and cost control	Statutory reporting
Input	• Individual enquiry of possible benefit permutations	• Initial selected benefits • Changes to selection • Entitlement parameters • Employment details	• Annual budget figures • Cost of benefit options	• Legislative changes/changes to parameters
Processing	• Validation of requested benefits against entitlement • Default to standard entitlements	• Generation of benefit statements • Maintenance of benefit history	• Monitoring against budget • Aggregation of total cost of benefits • Identification of benefits liable to – Tax – VAT – NIC	
Output	• Personal benefit illustrations • Warnings of exceeded entitlement	• Reports on benefit take up • Payslip breakdown • Annual individual benefits statements • Magnetic tape for payroll bureau		• VAT returns • NIC returns • P35 • P11D • P9D • P46 (Car)

Figure 18: Key functions of flexible benefits systems

¶1404

¶1405 Selecting a system – linking in

It is important to consider links with other systems such as:

- payroll;
- personnel;
- finance;
- other benefits administration (such as pensions).

These links could take the form of electronic links to existing company systems, or creating a new system with several functions of which flexible benefits is one. In whatever form, the flexible benefits system will operate within a framework which will include other links, not necessarily electronic. Figure 19 outlines this framework.

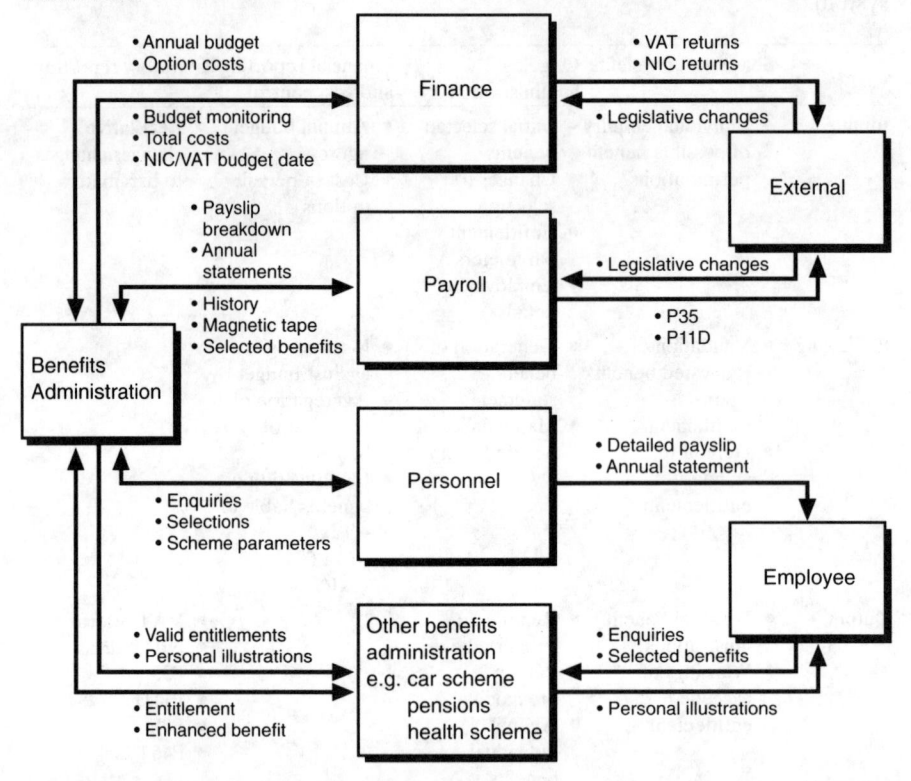

Figure 19: Relationships to other systems

The choice of an appropriate system will be strongly influenced by the framework within which it will exist. The scope for establishing efficient interfaces will therefore be a key factor in selection.

The creation of a system to administer flexible benefits provides an opportunity to review all personnel systems within an organisation, so careful examination of the framework in its entirety may have benefits (and costs) far beyond the introduction of flexible benefits per se.

¶1406 Preparation and procedures

Truly efficient administration relies on more than simply hardware and software. In order to gain maximum advantage from computerised administration of flexible benefits, an organisation also needs to have in place the right:

- people;
- procedures;
- documentation.

The people who will be involved in operating and administering the new system should be identified early on so they can be properly briefed and trained. They will need to have a good understanding of both the plan and the system. It will normally be best to involve the minimum number of people but a multi site company may need several people to support the plan in its different locations.

The procedures developed for using the system should specify who has access to information, and with what effect, and other security measures to preserve confidentiality. Procedures must also be designed for the efficient collection, recording, retrieval and dissemination of relevant information.

In close association with this development process, supporting documentation should be designed in a logical way, to facilitate transfer of information between manual and computerised sources. Consultation with staff who will operate the system is vital for this design process to be successful.

¶1407 Third-party administration

It is possible to contract out the administration of flexible benefits to a third party. Again, it is necessary to look carefully at interfaces (data and communication) and roles and procedures within the organisation. Whilst this type of arrangement can be used to avoid the administrative workload, it is necessary to ensure that clear responsibilities and points of contact are identified.

¶1408 Conclusion

Selection of appropriate software is the focus of administering flexible benefits efficiently and there is a range of possible solutions and systems. Appendix 3 sets out brief details of some of the systems which are available in the UK. To maximise the use of any new or enhanced system, however, suitable procedures must also be in place to ensure it is operated and understood fully by employees. Third-party administration is also available, thus enabling companies to focus on business issues as opposed to administrating benefit plans.

Our fourth case study illustrates how one UK company resolved its scheme administration issues.

Case Study 4: Colgate Palmolive – implementing a flexible benefits administration system

The organisation
Colgate Palmolive is one of the UK's leading FMCG companies which manufactures dental health and domestic products. It employs 700 staff in the UK at two sites. At Salford, the manufacturing site, there are 120 salaried staff and 430 waged staff. At the head office at Guildford, there are 150 salaried staff.

Busines issues/drivers for change
Colgate Palmolive have stated their aim to recruit high-calibre staff throughout the organisation. According to Laurence Moss, human resources manager at the Guildford head office, this can be difficult to achieve in the mature and competitive FMCG market. Reward packages are a major factor in the decision making process for potential candidates and, in Moss's view, a flexible benefits package offers a competitive edge in this respect.

The company thought it offered competitive compensation packages, but that the true value of the packages was not being clearly communicated to staff. So Colgate Palmolive considered introducing a flexible benefits plan to:

- underline and quantify the cash value of benefits to employees to demonstrate the competitiveness of its packages;
- emphasise the company's credo of empowerment: staff who determine their own package are more likely to be satisfied with it;

Corporate and Divisional management were favourable to the concept as a flexible benefits plan already existed in the US company. Staff communication was identified early on as a vital component of successful implementation.

Cost control, however, was not a factor in the decision. Senior management only stipulated that the plan be cost-neutral after start-up expenditure.

¶1408

The plan

The flexible benefits plan applies only to the company's 270 salaried staff.

There is a core package of benefits (including car, life assurance, long-term disability allowance). Staff may opt out of some of these, or reduce the level of benefit, gaining plan credits, and use these credits to 'flex-up' other benefits or simply to boost salary.

Under the new plan two new benefits are offered in addition to those offered previously. The total value of benefits remains as before so that the plan is cost neutral.

In order to avoid undue administrative complexity some benefits remain outside the flexible benefits plan. These include pensions and the stock ownership scheme.

Participants make their choices at year-end for the following flex year and these cannot be modified unless there are exceptional circumstances. The plan year runs from 6 April to 5 April.

Project approach

At the beginning of the project the company tested staff opinion at a focus group of senior management and a project team of seven key staff:

- legal director;
- two HR managers;
- communications manager;
- payroll manager;
- pensions manager;
- administrator.

A consultancy firm was used to facilitate the project and to advise on the design of the plan, and an independent consultant was hired to manage the project.

The project took place over a one-year period: the company says it would ideally have allowed two years, using a higher proportion of internal resources.

During the course of the implementation phase the company held several high-profile company presentations which were used to explain and sell the plan to staff. A design company prepared top quality briefing packs, reflecting the high priority Colgate Palmolive attaches to staff communications.

Generally, the project aimed for low complexity, with minimal change to existing systems. The project was given a high profile in the company and resources were allocated where necessary.

¶1408

Administration

The company initially carried out most of the plan administration manually using a spreadsheet to perform calculations. Denise Cross, who is responsible for the administration of the plan, says that the company quickly realised that the administrative effort required would add significantly to the costs of the project and that more sophisticated systems would be needed.

Colgate Palmolive rejected some of the specialist administration systems designed for the US market as inappropriate and generally too inflexible to accommodate their needs.

The system solution

The company finally settled on a specially designed system, fully integrated to their new PS2000 personnel system from Peterborough Software. The flexible benefits system maintains a record of individual staff choices, and the value of each choice. Choices are validated against the rules of the plan and the system produces paper-based reports for payroll administration and financial reporting systems.

Design and development of the system was carried out by Peterborough Software over a 10–12 week period at a cost of approximately £5,200.

Flexible benefit systems in the UK

Peterborough Software themselves take the view that, as the demand for flexible benefits systems is quite low, they would generally build systems on an individual basis. Clearly however, if they detected a rising demand or received a request from their user group then they would consider development of a more generic product which would be generally available to all their clients.

Other human resource system suppliers give a similar view. Whilst many offer systems originally designed for the US market, there is very little specifically designed for the UK.

Most suppliers however, would be pleased to discuss the possibility of building a bespoke system as an 'add-on' to a company's personnel system. Clearly though, such a development must be carefully planned, designed and tested before it is used for the plan administration.

Maintenance

One administrator at each site (Salford and Guildford) spends about one day per month adding new joiners, archiving leavers and passing on information to the underwriters. The workload increases towards the year end when the brochures are up-dated for the next flex year. The bulk of the administrative work peaks during the first quarter of the year when the choices are processed.

¶1408

In addition the administrators offer counselling to participants typically about tax and National Insurance issues, which obviously adds to their workload.

Conclusions
The plan has been received very positively by employees although Laurence Moss finds it difficult to gauge the true success of the project in attracting and retaining candidates in the current economic climate.

Both Laurence Moss and Denise Cross offer some sound words of advice for those considering the same route:

- Think through all aspects of the planning and timing of the project; Colgate Palmolive's experience suggests that such a project can be more time consuming than you anticipate.
- Set up arrangements for plan administration well in advance of the plan launch.
- Allow quality management time for considering how administration will be handled and for allocating roles and responsibilities.
- The introduction of the flexible benefits plan coincided with the implementation of a new personnel system. With hindsight, the company would have phased the two initiatives differently, or allowed more time.
- Simplicity is the key: the core system should be implemented first; complexity can be rolled-in (if absolutely necessary), but carries undue risk at the implementation stage.
- High priority should be given to staff communication throughout the lifecycle of the project.
- Significant cost reduction was not Colgate Palmolive's purpose in introducing flexible benefits. If cost control is your purpose in introducing flexible benefits, say so! You will be quickly found out if you do not.

¶1408

15 Telling Staff about the Flexible Benefits Plan

Executive summary

- Communication of a flex plan is a project in its own right requiring adequate planning and resources.
- Executive sponsorship is critical to success.
- It is critical to test employee reactions and understanding at several stages during the overall project, and to feed back progress to them.
- Plan the administration activities which will result from the communications exercise.
- The communications media need to be piloted before a full roll-out of the new plan. The roll-out itself will need to be phased.
- Match the media to the message – there are many innovative vehicles an organisation can use.
- Communicate to employees' partners, not just the workforce.
- Monitor employee response to the plan after implementation.

¶1501 The external context

Probably the first step in communications is not an internal exercise at all, but talking to other organisations which have introduced flexible benefits packages to learn from their experiences.

¶1502 Communication is a project in its own right

Communication is as much a key to success as a technically sound design. Once an organisation has decided to go ahead, communicating the plan is not an add-on to plan design and costing, but is an integral element of the overall project, and the organisation should put in place:

- a communications strategy;
- the communications objectives and success criteria;
- a project plan for the design, review and production of communications materials;

- a budget;
- a post project assessment of effectiveness.

Although communication is typically a small part of the overall cost of plan design and implementation, it is rarely given sufficient attention. Moreover, communication is not a one way process, and the process starts well before the design stage. Figure 20 illustrates the range of activities required.

Gain executive commitment / Test employee opinion / Set up a communications project team / Define the project plan	Research employee opinion / surveys / focus groups / Feed back the outcome	Test the design / Feed back the outcome	Pilot the communications media / Plan the communications administration	Rollout the full communications process

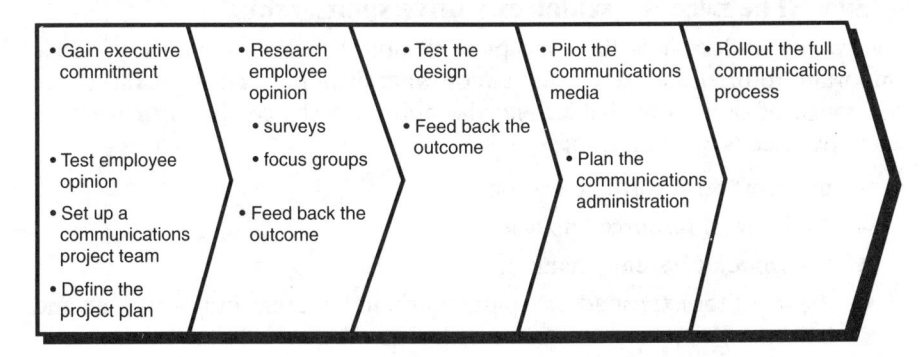

Figure 20: Communicating with staff

¶1503 Set up a communications project team

The change to flexible benefits will only be effective if all the interested parties communicate with each other throughout the process. The best way to achieve this is to establish a sub-project team to work alongside the main project team (see ¶103). There should be some common membership between the two project teams. The communications team should include some staff who will be affected by the new benefits packages so that they can suggest relevant communication messages and media. The team should also include, or at least have access to as necessary, legal and tax advisers to review all of the communications materials to ensure that they are technically sound.

¶1504 Testing the water

It is important to sound out opinions at the very earliest stages, from two specific target groups:

- the executive team whose sponsorship and overt commitment will be necessary throughout;
- Employees who are likely to receive the new benefits package.

It is a mistake to think that this process can take place overnight. To rush

¶1504

through at this stage may lead to a technically sound design, but one to which executives and staff have not 'bought-in'.

In the US a leading media agency D'Arcy Masius Benton & Bowles, Inc. are currently considering introducing flex. They have learnt from the experience of other organisations and are taking at least a year to sell the concept to the executive team and to staff.

¶1505 The need for senior executive sponsorship

Everybody understands the concept of flexible benefits – or do they? It is important to brief the executive team on what flexible benefits packages are, the range of options available, and the preferred choice. In particular, the executive needs to commit to:

- the short term cost implications;
- the internal resource implications;
- the scope of systems changes;
- the need for expert advice, particularly in the areas of pricing, tax and law;
- the organisation's philosophy towards winners and losers under the new arrangements, and how this stance fits with the corporate culture.

Only if the executive team can commit to the above and participate in the changes should the organisation proceed.

¶1506 Researching employees' opinions

Once commitment and sponsorship is assured, employee opinion must be tested. Employers often assume they are aware of employee likes and dislikes about the current benefits. At worst these assumptions need to be tested. At best the organisation should try to find out what staff really want. This can be done by a questionnaire to all, or a sample of the staff who might be affected. It may be appropriate to start the research process with senior staff first so that they are able to sponsor the change as more junior staff are brought in to the process.

¶1507 A two-way communication process

An important step in the process is to provide sufficient understanding of flexible benefits packages and the organisation's possible approach, so that staff know what they are being asked their views on and why. Focus groups which allow two-way communication are a more effective way to explore employees' views than a written questionnaire.

As an introduction to the focus group it is important to describe to employees:

- the reasons for the change to benefits provision;
- the organisation's objectives for the changes;
- an outline of flexible benefits;
- the organisation's philosophy towards winners and losers;
- how the changes will be introduced.

Thereafter it is important to *listen* to what the employees say about the current arrangements, and their views on the proposed changes and the 'hot buttons', the things which excite employees about the possible change. Figure 21 lists the topics which need to be explored.

¶1508 Tell employees whether the project will proceed

At this point, the organisation needs to decide whether or not to go ahead. If the existing benefits plan meets the organisation's objectives, if benefit costs are not rising (or are unlikely to rise), and employees are content with their current benefits, it may not be appropriate to proceed. A specific decision should be made, the project should not just wander along because it has been started. Communicate the decision when it has been made.

¶1509 Consult employees at every stage in the project

Possibly using additional resources for detailed work, the project team can work together to design the new plan, taking account of what the affected employees said at the earlier consultation stages. At this stage, staff should ideally be consulted again about the potential design of the plan. The topics to be explored are set out in Figure 21.

At the feasibility stage:
- Employee morale and motivation
- Organisational tolerance for a resistance to change
- Understanding of current benefits arrangements:
  - range of benefits (including spouse/partner)
  - cost/value of benefit
- Satisfaction with current arrangements
- Understanding of the flexible benefits concepts
- Benefits over which employees would like to exercise choice
- Willingness to contribute from salary to top up employer's contributions
- Preferred methods of communication of changes.

> At the design stage:
> - Understanding of proposed design
> - Areas of satisfaction/dissatisfaction
> - Propensity to move away from current arrangements
> - User-friendliness of proposed administration
> - Effectiveness of proposed communications methods.

Figure 21: Topics for employee attitude survey

Once again it is important to listen at this stage, and if necessary to:
- go no further;
- change direction;
- adjust the plan design.

The final design of the plan should be communicated to, and agreed upon, by:
- the executive team;
- benefits personnel;
- internal or external tax, legal and actuarial advisers;
- benefits providers.

To make the decision to implement flexible benefits, those listed above should have the full knowledge that staff will support the plan, or that the organisation has a clearly defined plan to manage areas of resistance.

The pre- and post-design surveys are the mechanisms for obtaining that knowledge but will in themselves raise staff expectations for change. It is important to feed back a message about the overall direction the organisation intends to take.

¶1510 Pilot the communications media

Before the full communications exercise (described in ¶1512) it is important to pilot:
- the communication methods;
- the plan paperwork, and election process.

¶1511 Plan the communications administration

A lot of thought often goes into the design of the election forms, but little on how:
- forms will be distributed;

- forms will be collected;
- non-returns will be followed up;
- errors and omissions will be processed;
- enrolment choices will be confirmed.

¶1512 Communication is a phased process

Only now is the organisation ready to communicate to the whole of the target population (although many organisations regard this step as the only stage in the communications process). However, it is not a single stage. There is a need to:

- dispel rumours;
- reassure employees of the plan's advantages;
- generate interest and support, which will vary by individual's life stage and style;
- educate;
- convey the timing and the extent of information available;
- support the legal and tax positions being taken;
- ensure that the formal and informal communications match.

This cannot be done at one session, whatever media are used, and serial delivery will be necessary.

¶1513 Key messages

The key messages to communicate to staff are:

- flexible benefits is a key aspect of good human resource management in the 1990s;
- the company's objectives in introducing the plan;
- how the plan works and enough information to make choices, including specific details on:
    (a) operating framework,
    (b) benefits menu,
    (c) points allocation,
    (d) benefits pricing,
    (e) election period;
- procedures for making the choice, handling the trade-offs, and what to do if you change your mind;
- numerous worked examples;
- assistance is available to individuals.

¶1513

¶1514 Match the media to the message

Employees' perceptions will be influenced by the way in which the message is conveyed, and a mismatch between the media and the message is a common problem. Similarly, it is essential to allow ample time between communicating the new plan, and requiring employees to make a choice.

Although communications research shows that face-to-face communications with an employee's own boss are most effective, with a change as complex as flexible benefits it will be vital to provide written materials. However, too many organisations are over-reliant on this method. Figure 22 illustrates the variety of media available, together with their relative advantages and disadvantages.

Options	Advantages	Disadvantages
Departmental briefings/ cascade	• Managers prime communicators • Managers key to feeding back questions and issues to senior management • Can be video taped for absentees	• Managers' current communication skills • Messages can be inconsistent especially if a cascade process is used • Managers may be 'losers' and therefore lack commitment • Insufficient knowledge
Large conference(s)	• Motivational events • Definite launch of flexible benefits plan • Positions senior management as communicators	• Remote from work • Cost • Disruptive to the business
One to one counselling	• Specific to each employee	• Cost • Time required
Company newsletter	• Potentially can provide a consistent message	• Newsletter is not always widely read • Not normally used for such purposes
Flexible benefits plan newsletter	• Specifically designed for communicating information about project • Consistency • Rapid dissemination	• Erratic publication

Options	Advantages	Disadvantages
Video	• Consistency • If done well, is professional	• Cost/time to produce • Relies on managers to hold local discussions to increase relevance • Need to have something definite to say, i.e. more than principles • Familiar medium to audience
Notice-boards	• Good reminders of key points • Consistent message • Can be localised	• Could become out of date • Need to allocate responsibility
Personnel department	• Effective communication channel	• Could undermine position of managers • Stretched resources
Information packs	• Consistency • Information to hand • Rapid dissemination	• Time/cost to produce high quality product
Focus groups/feedback sessions	• Useful for testing response and comprehension • Can deepen understanding of areas of concern	• Captures views of most vocal • Time consuming
Question and answer sheets	• Relatively quick current response • Can enable less confident to raise questions	• Can become bureaucratic process • Answers not necessarily credible, impersonal • Large workload at centre
Training/workshops	• Consistent message • Allows time to practise knowledge and skills	• Cost/time involved

¶1514

Options	Advantages	Disadvantages
Directors' briefings	• Useful forum to raise issues • Specifically focused on top ground • Ownership at the top of the organisation	• Must be carefully structured to ensure productive use is made of time • Time consuming
Telephone helpline	• Quick response • Enable less confident to raise questions • Useful especially during election period • Suppliers may also provide helplines	• Time/cost to resource
Pay slip stuffers	• Reaches all eligible staff	• Often left unread
Personalised benefit statements	• Sets out each individual's situation	• Time/cost to produce
Voicemail	• Easy to use from work or home • Can be set up to take direct input • Can be used by employee or partner	• Cost to set up if not already in use • Cannot answer interactive questions
Multi media	• Secure system which can hold all individual and scheme details • Can be set up to take direct input • Can be used by employee and partner • Can communicate corporate messages and detailed data	• Cost to set up and maintain • Probably only provided to populous locations • Need for hard copy information to back up system

Figure 22: Communicating with staff

¶1514

¶1515 Partners are part of the decision-making process
In many cases, the employer will not be communicating only with its employees, but often with their partners or spouses as well. These people have a personal interest in the benefits choices made. Some organisations find it useful to invite partners to the briefing or advice sessions.

¶1516 Monitor the plan
Once the new plan is in place it is important to continue regular soundings and assessments. One year's enrolment forms can give an indication of which benefits employees favour, and likely choices for the future. However, in the first year of a plan, selection often mirrors the previous benefits package and may not be a reliable guide.

¶1517 Summary
To introduce a flexible benefits package successfully requires close attention to the communications questions so familiar to human resources managers in other fields of their work – what? who? when? why? how?

Our fifth case study describes how a media company approached the communications task, and used some of its own business methods internally.

> **Case Study 5: Saatchi & Saatchi North America Inc: the Lifecare Adviser – using communications to the full**
>
> Saatchi & Saatchi NA Inc. is the north American subsidiary of a major advertising and media corporation, reporting to its parent in the UK. The majority of the employees are young, single professionals with an average age of 34. In other words, an employee group unlikely to spend their time reading volumes of paper communications about pensions and long-term disability. Like many US companies, it needed to control the costs of its health care plans, and in 1987 introduced a limited flexible benefits programme. However, the plan was not greatly successful. The exodus of employees from the staff health care scheme to health maintenance organisations (HMOs), together with other aspects of the design, turned the scheme into a money loser rather than a cost controller.
>
> *Lessons learned*
> With hindsight, Saatchi reviewed where it had gone wrong. There were undoubtedly some pricing and design faults, but there were also aspects of the communication project which had not worked:
>
> - the plan was put together in just three months which meant that Saatchi did not have as much time as it would have liked to communicate with staff;

- since there was no staff input to the initial plan, the final design did not optimally fulfil the needs of plan participants.

Objectives for the new plan
During the plan's existence Saatchi had acquired a number of companies, each with its own flex plan. Saatchi wanted to rationalise so that it could offer one single plan. It was time for a major re-think, and Saatchi defined the objectives for a new plan:

- to educate employees about the value of their benefits, and the cost to Saatchi;
- to design a plan which would meet the needs of the workforce, and so gain their commitment;
- to control costs;
- to attract employees away from HMOs and into the Saatchi-funded indemnity plans so that Saatchi could benefit from an excellent claims record (because of the young age profile) spreading the risk through a larger group would give Saatchi the chance to control the annual premium increases and thereby indirectly benefit its personnel;
- to aim to reinsure by the mid 1990s to allow flexibility outside state regulations.

Consulting employees
Saatchi invested a great deal of time and resources in the pre-design consultation stage to find out what employees wanted. Employees took part in 22 focus groups which took place throughout the country, and 40 per cent of employees responded to an attitude survey, a very good response rate from media employees.

Employees' views
The results of the consultation process showed that staff did not know:

- what benefits they were eligible for;
- how to use the benefits, or in what circumstances;
- how much their benefits cost (they only knew how much they paid as contributions).

In terms of what employees wanted, the key messages were:

- staff did not want any deductions from their salary to pay for benefits;
- employees wanted disability insurance, and a physical examination every year;
- above all, employees wanted more choice to suit their needs.

¶1517

Demonstrating commitment

The focus groups took place a year before the new plan was to be implemented. However, just three months into the consultation process and a long time before implementation, Saatchi changed the disability benefit. The company proved their commitment to a plan based on employees concerns and desires, and proved that it was listening to what the staff were saying.

Saatchi endorsed its corporate culture and included some paternal elements in the plan. The indemnity plan is a core benefit, so employees are automatically covered, even if they make no further elections. Every employee is given the same number of lifecare dollars to spend, irrespective of status or family circumstances. Single employees receive a full range of benefits without making any contributions.

Communicating the plan

Although design is inevitably complex and technical, the major issue for Saatchi was how to communicate the new plan to a group of young creative people, who frequently travel out of the office, and who are unlikely to read newsletters or written details about new benefits arrangements. Saatchi drew on its own skills as a business, and designed the communications project as an advertising campaign – posters, brief eye-catching pamphlets and short memos announced the key features of the plan.

This left the problem of how to get staff to read sufficient detail to make their benefits elections, and to register their choices with the personnel department.

In the early stages, Saatchi used an interactive telephone system – the Lifecare Information Line, which provided a paperless enrolment system. Employees entered their own data and computer coding prevented invalid choices. The computer system then automatically produced employee statements.

Saatchi also produced a video for staff to take home and share with their partners who were very often influential in the benefits choice.

Using technology

The next stage of communications was more sophisticated. The Lifecare Adviser is a booth with a screen and keyboard like that of a bank ATM or 'hole-in-the-wall' machine. Using the headsets for total privacy, a multimedia narrated display guides the employee through all aspects of the flex package. The system allows employees to model different options and contribution levels within their eligibility criteria. An important decision was to make the recordings in Saatchi's own facilities.

In Phase II of the Lifecare Adviser introduced in July 1992, Saatchi

¶1517

implemented an intelligent system linked up to a data server with the payroll and pensions systems. Now the system holds all the personal data, so the employee has only to enter changes or the 'what if' data. As a result there is only a limited requirement for administrative support from the personnel and benefits departments. Their principle role is to update the data servers so that new information is displayed in the kiosks.

The system is secured by use of employee's social security number and an allocated PIN number, which can also be used by the employee's partner.

Post-implementation
Saatchi continues to monitor its flex package. A few months after implementation employees attended further focus groups. The research confirmed how much partners influence the choice and take-up of benefits and Saatchi recognises how important it is to target them with the communications.

Saatchi now has a successful flex plan to which employees are committed. They have one of the most sophisticated systems support which does everything possible to facilitate election and benefits changes. The company planned its communications programme thoroughly, and exploited a full range of media.

The key lesson
Technical design is only one facet of a successful flex plan, managing the human element is often the most difficult.

¶1517

16 Implementation of Flexible Compensation at CIGNA Employee Benefits

Summary

This final chapter pulls together all the key issues that need to be considered for a flex plan from its inception through implementation to monitoring of the final plan.

The main part of this chapter is a case study written by Keith Wilkinson, Human Resources Manager at CIGNA Employee Benefits. He takes us through the process CIGNA followed in putting their own plan in place.

¶1601 About CIGNA

CIGNA re-launched in the UK marketplace in July 1991. As an international company specialising in risk-based employee benefits, particularly medical and managed care, but also providing group health, life, long-term disability, and dental insurance, it was keen to ensure that whilst in its infancy it would demonstrate a credibility for innovation and have a 'leading edge' in the growth of the flexible benefits market in the 1990s.

The re-focusing of CIGNA was not only achieved from a marketing perspective, but during 1991 and 1992 the business has been 're-engineered'. This business re-processing has resulted in a heavy investment in skills development, creating self-directed, empowered teams, centred on providing high-quality customer service. With this additional increase in responsibilities, the company wanted to demonstrate its concern for the individual needs of its employees, and thus provide a benefits package that in its delivery would provide the basis for total flexibility.

¶1602 Preparation for flex – employee survey

Recognising the limited amount of resources available, and wanting to ensure that we were able to gather information from the employees regarding their understanding and value of the current benefits package, without any

¶1602

pre-conceived ideas, we retained external benefits consultants to undertake an employee attitude survey.

The survey was conducted by using focus groups in both our main employee bases in Greenock and London, with two groups in each location, both providing a complete cross-section of employees from clerical through to professional.

The results of this survey revealed that, throughout the organisation, there was a poor awareness of both the range of benefits provided by us as employers, and also the cost of those benefits to the organisation. This was a clear challenge to us, as the majority of benefits provided by the organisation were those which we were seeking to provide in the employee benefits marketplace.

Additional issues that were raised through the focus groups were the relevancy of benefits; inadequate communication of the salary structure; low awareness of the CIGNA job evaluation process; and concern that the recognised step levels of progression were being eroded as the organisation flattened its structure. Finally, the survey revealed a lack of trust in the communication from line management.

¶1603 The external consultant

The value of utilising an independent consultant for this exercise cannot be underestimated, as it has brought to the surface issues which extend far beyond the scope of the original brief, however with an awareness of these points we have not only been able to implement a flexible compensation programme, but to do it successfully, addressing all the underlying issues raised by the staff.

¶1604 Plan design

As a company involved in providing risk insurance products to the employee benefit marketplace, we provided a significant range of employer paid benefits. Detailed below are the benefits provided prior to the introduction of flex.

Existing benefits

Private medical insurance	Employer paid, to all employees with coverage provided at provincial scale. Further options available to provide coverage for spouse, family at provincial level and all covers at London level.
Group life	Employer paid, providing a benefit of three times basic salary, and an additional option available at employee cost for a fourth multiple.

Long-term disability	Employer paid, providing a benefit of 60 per cent of gross salary after six months continuous absence from work due to ill health.
Dental insurance	Employer paid, providing comprehensive cover for preventative treatment and subsidised cost of restorative work, both to NHS and private dentists.
Mortgage subsidy	Employer paid, to all staff over the age of 18 with one year's service, a cash subsidy reducing the interest rate on the first £15,000 of mortgage from the current rate (with a maximum of 13 per cent) down to 3.5 per cent, and on the second £15,000 of mortgage from the current rate (with a maximum of 13 per cent) to 10 per cent. Mortgages in excess of £30,000 were not taken into account for this purpose.
Meal allowance	Employer-paid contributions towards cost of lunch – annual rate of £348.
Company cars	Both 'needs' and 'perquisite' with a limited range of models, and no provision for those who did not spend their full allowance, or others who did not require a company car.
Non-contributory pension scheme	Employer paid, applicable to all employees over the age of 21, the scheme is defined benefit, on the basis of 60ths of completed years of service.
Personal accident insurance	Employee paid, providing various levels of cover if permanent injury or accidental death sustained.

In working with the consultants on the plan design, the main issues were:

- productive communication of benefit value;
- the ability to meet the real needs of employees;
- to ensure employees were able to make good choices.

Although these points sound simple, the plan almost fell down due to the initial concept of including the pension scheme within the flex programme. Also, we were aware that the provision of choice needed to be matched by the provision of a good understanding of how to make the right choices.

¶1604

Flexible benefits
In order to maintain a good level of insured coverage for our employees, and to demonstrate commitment to our own product range, the company took the choice to remove some benefits altogether, have a central core package and provide a full range of flexible options.

Benefits removed
Two benefits that the company ceased to provide at this time were mortgage subsidy and meal allowance.

Mortgage subsidy had been identified as both administratively intensive, and also resulting in fluctuating expense levels to the organisation. It was also considered by senior management to be unfair on a significant number of employees, who for a variety of reasons, did not own their own property.

The meal allowance was a historical benefit that resulted from having a head office with staff restaurant facilities, and a number of branches with no such facility, and therefore a cash benefit was provided to compensate. With the relocation of the company from our former head office in Reigate, Surrey to a new headquarters in Greenock, Scotland where no staff restaurant facilities were available, all employees throughout the organisation were provided with a meal allowance, and therefore the differential no longer existed.

In removing these benefits, the company provided a cash substitute termed the 'flex fund'. To arrive at this element an audit of the current level of mortgage subsidy payable to all those receiving the benefit was taken, and the average amount was paid to all staff, where previously only 70 per cent of staff received the benefit. Additionally, £350 was provided to the flex fund to cover the loss of the meal allowance.

Core benefits
The core benefits are those benefits which all employees must purchase from their flex fund to a basic level or benefit. They are:

- private medical insurance,
- life cover at three times salary,
- long term disability,
- dental insurance.

The premium cost of each of these insurances is added to the value of the flex fund, but must be spent in purchasing each of the benefits.

Flexible options
Private medical insurance   In line with the previous range of choices that were available on this benefit, employees could

¶1604

	opt to include spouse, spouse and children, or children at either provincial or London rates.
Group life	The option of increasing cover by a fourth multiple remains.
Long term disability	Choices available were increased by allowing options of a 3 per cent or 5 per cent escalation of benefit as an indexation against erosion of benefit by inflation.
Dental insurance	A voluntary scheme was created providing benefit cover for spouses.
Holidays	All employees were allowed to either buy or sell up to a maximum of five days holiday, the cost of each day calculated as 1/265th of annual salary. The parameters in which the sale or purchase were allowed was that an employee must still have 15 days holiday, and cannot have any more than 30 days.
Health screening	The opportunity to purchase well woman/well man or a full health screening was made available.
Personal accident	The previous range of choices that were available through the voluntary personal accident scheme continued to be offered.
Child accident	This scheme offers enhanced benefits on personal accident cover for children.
Company car	The opportunity for perquisite car users was provided to buy up or sell down or even come out of the company car scheme. For those who were need users, they had the opportunity to buy up in their choice of company car. These options are being phased in as holders of the company cars renew their existing car at either the four year renewal or 60,000 miles.
Private petrol	For those who are allocated a company car, the opportunity to provide for private petrol was included. This provides a tax efficient opportunity for company car holders with high private mileage usage.

¶1604

Pensions

The decision to omit the pension scheme from the programme in the first year enabled all financial advice around the decision making process to be handled in-house.

¶1605 Implementation

Conceptual thinking for our flexible compensation scheme at CIGNA took place in July and August of 1991. As a result, the Employee Benefits Consultants were contacted in late August 1991. Following preliminary discussions surrounding the nature of the project, focus groups were held in mid October, with the report of recommendations for next steps presented in November.

Over the following months, the basis of a flexible benefits plan was created in conjunction with the senior management of CIGNA Employee Benefits and the Consultants.

This plan was then distributed to the UK senior management on 1 March 1992, with a senior management meeting that ratified the plan design on 12 March. The speed of the decision-making process involved here was enhanced by the participation of many managers in the creation of the plan design.

Within a week of the decision, all staff were informed that a major change would take place to the provision of their benefits towards the end of the year, and that under these changes they would be able to make a greater range of choices that would be more suited to their individual needs. No specific details of the plan design were included, but a commitment was made to further communication on a regular basis.

¶1606 Communication

To ensure the problem surrounding credibility of line management communication was thoroughly addressed, in mid May all line managers throughout the company were briefed in detail on the flexible benefits plan, the benefits to be included, the means by which the choices were to be made, and the basis upon which the flex fund had been agreed.

On completion of this exercise, all employees were provided with a handout on flex explaining how the plan works, core benefits, and the flex choices. Although not explaining every benefit in detail, the handout provided a full outline of the flex plan.

During June, the relevant personal details were downloaded from the HR system, and uploaded into the flexible benefits administration system that had been acquired by CIGNA for the purpose of administering the plan. These details were then validated, and the preparation of preference forms and all communications materials was completed.

At the beginning of July, all employees in every location received on their desks, inside a small box, a dice. It did not take long for the inquisitive to arrive at the conclusion that the dice was loaded.

Three days later, a booklet which explained in detail the plan design arrived on the desk of each employee, under the title 'Loading the Dice in Your Favour'. The booklet itself had been designed to be readable and interesting – a move away from the flexible benefits handbooks produced in the US which are comprehensive manuals requiring considerable time and effort to understand.

Whilst the booklet contained considerable detail around each benefit, it did not hold any specific details with regard to cost for any particular benefit. These were included in an insert flap at the rear of the booklet. The advantage this provided was to tailor each book to each individual, and prevented any undue criticism that may have arisen surrounding company cars, private petrol, etc.

¶1607 Understanding the choices made

A fundamental issue that needed to be dealt with was how to help the employee make good choices surrounding their benefit needs. In order to address this issue, a board game was provided to every employee four days after the distribution of the booklets. 'Reflexion', the board game, presented unusual lifestyles that the employees had to adopt, and choose the benefits that they felt applicable to a person with that lifestyle and circumstances, including salary, holidays, and flex fund.

The game then required them to move around the board, and in so doing they came across different aspects of life which we all face, including holiday, council tax, purchase of a major household item. On top of this there would be 'windfalls' and 'disasters' set around personal circumstances that would require hospital treatment, dental treatment, personal accident cover, etc. The purpose of this was to ensure that all employees had a strong grasp of the issues surrounding the benefit choices they had made for the lifestyle they had adopted, but in a format that was amusing and entertaining, and could be easily taken back to their own homes, where clearly there was a significant impact surrounding the decisions they were to make on the flexible benefits programme.

In the second week in July, all employees attended major presentations of the flexible benefits programme. These commenced with the distribution of the preference forms, which they were to complete, indicating their choice of benefits. Each form was personalised, with full details of name, date of birth, NI number, number of days holiday entitlement, cost of each individual day's holiday, and value of flex fund.

The presentation also discussed the tax implications surrounding the choices and also how the flex fund had been calculated, and the opportunities that this change in benefits provided for employees.

Flexible Benefits

At the end of the presentation, aware of possible scepticism, each presentation concluded by playing 'Reflexion', further endorsing our commitment to help employees understand the nature of the choices they would be making in their selection of preferences.

¶1608 Helplines

As the enrolment period spanned the summer, there was the opportunity for individual counselling sessions, discussion with line managers, and discussion with the human resources department. All forms were to be returned to the human resources department by the end of August, and in the first two weeks of September, test runs were completed for payroll deductions, preference forms were screened and confirmation of benefit statements were distributed to all employees indicating whether their preferences had been approved or required alteration. Copies of the confirmation of benefit statements were then returned, signed, to human resources in order that payroll authorisation was completed.

On 1 October 1992, the CIGNA Employee Benefits Flexible Benefits Programme went live, and the following month an in-house survey was completed by the marketing function to assess the effectiveness of the communications process.

The results of this revealed a significantly enhanced understanding of benefit value, and the range of benefits available to all employees. Whilst there was an element of criticism regarding the amount that had been spent on the communications exercise, including the dice and the game, overall it was felt that these items had brought about a greater understanding of the issues involved in benefit selection.

¶1609 Benefit shifts

Looking at three particular benefits that were provided both pre- and post-flex, it is clear that the value of benefits, both in cost terms and in risk cover, were better appreciated and taken up by employees, the following table being a clear indication of the impact upon Private Medical Insurance, Group Life, and Personal Accident Cover.

Benefit	Pre-flex take up		Post-flex take up	
	Number	*Value (£)*	*Number*	*Value (£)*
Medical upgrade	65		81	
Supplementary life	47	853,600	71	1,417,500
Voluntary personal accident	103	7,640,000	157	10,880,000

¶1610 Employer advantages

The introduction of flexible benefits for CIGNA has provided an excellent opportunity to improve communications between management and staff, not just through the programme, but as a result of the employee attitude survey it has led to open, regular, effective communication at all levels of the organisation.

The in-house survey has revealed that the programme is seen to meet individual needs and has increased employee perception of the value of benefits provided by the company.

Although provision of employee benefits in the UK is not currently suffering from the spiralling prices incurred in the US, introduction of the flexible benefits programme does provide the platform for cost control if such a situation were to occur in the UK. Rather than withdrawal of benefit, a move to shared cost on a percentage basis between employee/employer can easily be achieved through flexible benefits.

The introduction of flexible benefits in 1992 is not on a finalised rigid format, and it is the intention of the company to increase the range of benefits that are available to employees in subsequent years. For 1993, we are considering areas around dependant day-care, provision of home use PC equipment, and inclusion of the pension scheme. The ability to enhance the plan is endless with suggestions already coming from employees on further issues they would like to see included.

¶1611 Employee advantages

The most outstanding of these has been the ability to tailor an individual package to meet specific personal needs. Employees at all levels throughout the organisation have indicated that this is of considerable value to them. Further, the opportunity to review the benefit selection annually enables employees to change benefit selection to meet major lifestyle changes, for example moving house, starting a family, change of marital status.

Not to be understated, is the fact that employees now understand the cost to the company of the benefits that they are provided with throughout the course of the year. This has certainly led to a development in employee loyalty, with a resulting reduction in employee turnover.

¶1612 Overview

For us as a company, the implementation of a flexible benefits programme has enabled us to develop a total compensation strategy, which enables us to take a clear look at all the cost issues surrounding our benefit provision. Within this strategy we now have the opportunity to control costs, enhance benefits, and develop a comprehensive and interesting benefit programme that provides all employees with the opportunity to select against their personal preferences.

Benefit administration has been reduced with the removal of the mortgage subsidy, and the movement to a fixed approach to benefit provision for all employees. Also the removal of mortgage subsidy has provided us with the opportunity to demonstrate our determination to move towards a single status approach as an organisation.

In conclusion, and with the opportunity of hindsight, there are no significant changes we would make to the development of the plan that we now have in place. The move to flexible benefits has been an extension of the culture which has been developing within CIGNA over the past few years, where there has been an increased emphasis on personal responsibility and decision making through the re-engineering process.

It further demonstrates that as an organisation, we are at the leading edge of benefit practice in the UK, have demonstrated the ability to deliver innovative benefit packages to employees, and also understand all the issues surrounding the underwriting of flexible benefits in the risk insurance marketplace.

¶1613 The future for flex – a comment from the editors

In summary, we at Coopers & Lybrand think that flex will become one of the driving forces behind employee motivation and retention in the 1990s. Our aim throughout this book has been to demonstrate clearly the value of flex to the employer and to enable employers to understand what it is they need to do in order to make flex work for them.

The role of the consultant is a necessary one and we have highlighted the areas where we can add value to the process whilst leaving the control in the hands of those who have to live with the consequences of the decision – you.

Appendix 1: Cash or Cars

Avoiding the tax traps
A properly constructed plan under which directors or employees have the right to take cash allowances in lieu of cars should not give rise to any untoward tax consequences. That is to say, those who take company cars will be taxed merely by reference to the cars which they take and those who take cash alternatives will be taxed by reference to the cash alternative which each takes. In addition, those taking company cars will give rise to Class 1A NIC in the hands of the company, but not Class 1 contributions; and those taking cash will give rise to Class 1 contributions only.

Frequency of choice
There are, however, limits to how frequently the choice can be exercised by an individual. If he or she is in receipt of a company car, the Inland Revenue will, probably correctly, argue that he or she is taxable on the higher of the scale charge and the cash alternative which should be taken if he or she is allowed to change his or her selection more often than once a year. It is normal practice that cars are allocated to employees for longer periods, normally three or four years. There should be no problem, as long as that remains the rule.

There is no tax difficulty if the employer allows those who have opted for the cash alternative to change their minds at any given time. As a matter of administrative convenience, the employer will wish to limit the number of occasions on which the employee can opt for a car but there are no tax issues to take into account.

The importance of contractual arrangements
The employer also needs to be sure that the contractual arrangements with the employees are dealt with carefully. The danger to avoid is that, if individuals have a high salary, part of which they can apply in payment for a car, there will be VAT on the amount used to take that car, there will be income tax and Class I NIC on the higher salary, there will be a scale charge and Class 1A NIC on the car and, quite possibly, no relief for the amount which the individuals are applying in order to take the car.

What must therefore be avoided is individuals having a contractual right to a relatively high salary which they are entitled to apply in part to taking a company car. It is perfectly acceptable if they have a lower salary with the right to either a car or a cash supplement in addition. The commercial difference between the two may be small but the tax difference is substantial and it is a matter of ensuring that the contractual documentation, in contracts of employment, letters announcing salary changes, staff handbooks or payslips are all in line with the contractual situation which the employer is attempting to establish.

Setting the cash alternative

If the employer intends to pay individuals an amount equal to, or calculated by reference to, the cost to the company of providing the car to which the individual would otherwise be entitled, the cash alternative would be the total cost for the benchmark car to which an employee is entitled, including interest, depreciation, contract-hire rentals and inclusive of any VAT which the organisation is unable to recover. In addition to the costs the employer needs to include an allowance for costs which are not covered by the contract-hire rental, such as insurance and road tax and add Class 1A NIC.

Which motoring costs to compare

Finally, there is the question of what motoring costs to compare. Possible options include the current estimate of costs of a car acquired now or some standard figures, provided by the company providing the cars or taken from one of the company car publications. Either approach is based on the assumption that the employer is paying no more than market average rates for acquiring and maintaining its cars. Checking that assumption could itself be a useful exercise.

There are ways of saving money by changing the legal nature of the method of procurement without affecting the level of service received from the company providing the cars.

For employees, you will need to bear in mind that their costs, particularly for depreciation and insurance, may vary significantly from the employer's and it may be appropriate to take account of this in the calculations.

Taking account of National Insurance contributions

It is also necessary to take into account the Class 1 NIC liability which will arise on the payment of the extra salary. It is illegal to charge employees with employer's NIC, but to have a formula, which in practice takes acount of NIC, is entirely in order. For example, the employer may ensure that staff were entitled to a figure of 90 per cent of the computed cost of a company car, but to take 100 per cent less employer's NIC would be wrong.

Cost of administration

Most organisations do not make an adjustment for administration on the grounds that, even though there is a higher administrative cost associated with cars than there is with cash, those costs are relatively fixed unless the fleet is substantially reduced.

Dealing with business mileage

It is also important to consider how to deal with business mileage. If the cash alternative covers the full cost of the company car, it would be double-counting to pay a full reimbursement for business mileage. A small premium over the petrol costs would be more appropriate. This is, however, costly in terms of NIC (Class 1 NIC would be payable on the extra salary) and individuals would obtain income tax relief only by making a rather complex claim in their tax returns. The alternative of paying a lower additional cash allowance but higher mileage rates is more efficient but may make it more difficult to achieve equity between different employees.

The resulting figures, adjusted for the somewhat complex rules under which corporation tax relief is available for the costs of the car, will be the after-tax equivalent of the additional cash allowance which the employer would offer.

Treatment of the cash allowance

It is necessary to consider the relationship between the cash allowance, which would be paid to staff not taking a car, and salary-related benefits. The plan documentation would need to make it clear whether the cash allowance was or was not eligible to be taken into account as salary for the purposes of the company's pension scheme and any other salary-related benefits such as bonus, overtime or share schemes. The rules of the related benefit plans, such as the pension scheme or share scheme, should also be checked to ensure that the consistency is achieved.

If the cash allowance should be taken into account in fixing certain salary-related benefits, it may be appropriate to reduce the level of allowance payable accordingly. Most employers take the view that cars are ignored in calculating salary-related benefits and that the cash allowance should similarly be ignored.

Frequency of payment of the cash allowance

The employer will also need to determine the frequency of payment of the cash allowance. It could be annually and the employee can choose each year whether to retain the cash allowance or take a car. On the other hand, an annual revision would in the second and subsequent years mean that the salary alternative was more than the cost of the car the employee could have taken in the first year. Many of a car's costs are effectively fixed at the time of acquisition. A more equitable approach might be to set the cash allowance somewhat below the actual cost of providing the car. Annual increases would then allow the total costs of the cash alternative to equate more closely with the lifetime (or total lease) costs of providing a car.

Appendix 2: The Tax Treatment of Flexible Compensation

Introduction

The purpose of this appendix is to discuss how flexible compensation is treated under current UK tax law. The appendix covers the position from the point of view of the employee, dealing with income tax. It covers National Insurance contributions (NIC) and value added tax (VAT). It does not deal with the employer's position under Schedule D. Its contents are as follows:

- Income tax
- Value added tax
- National Insurance contributions
- Flexible compensation and notional salaries
- The legal relationship.

Throughout the text of this book we have taken care to refer to the individual as 'he or she'. In this appendix however we have used the single word 'he' to mean 'the employee', since the number of times that the pronoun is used makes it impractical to do otherwise.

Income tax

The tax treatment of flexible compensation flows naturally from the principles which underlie the tax treatment of remuneration. The relevant points are set out in the following paragraphs.

An individual is taxed on the emoluments from his employment (ICTA 1988, s.19(1)). The term 'emoluments' is defined as including not only wages and salaries but also any profits or perquisites (ICTA 1988, s.131(1)).

Nature of the emoluments

The first point to determine is what the employee received. Did he receive a perquisite or a benefit in kind from his employer or did he receive salary which he had applied in paying his employer for a service or benefit? A significant amount of case law has arisen around this issue. The best known case is that of *Heaton v Bell*.

In the case of *Heaton v Bell* ((1969) 46 TC 211), a litho machine minder of John Waddington Limited gave up a proportion of his gross salary, probably £2 13s 6d per

Appendix 2: The Tax Treatment of Flexible Compensation

week from June 1964, in exchange for a company car (an Austin A40). Although it is the leading case on flexible compensation, *Heaton* v *Bell* was in fact decided on the basis that Mr Bell had never given up his gross salary in the first place. Although the contract of employment was apparently changed, Mr Bell's payslip showed his old, higher, salary continuing and his car rental shown as a deduction. The old wage formed the basis of his overtime and allowances. Despite the fact that the deduction would not have been charged in a week when Mr Bell was ill (and thus unpaid), the House of Lords in a majority judgement held that the facts of the case indicated that his real gross pay had not changed and the deduction was just a rent-charge. For example, his payslips and the basis on which overtime was calculated were evidence that he had remained entitled to the gross salary and had applied it as rent for the car.

Choice and tax

The effect of this and other cases is as follows. If, before an individual joins a company, he is given a choice of either one level of salary with benefits in kind or a higher level of salary with more modest or non-existent benefits in kind, this once-for-all choice of cash or a benefit is, on being offered to an individual, no more than the negotiation of his package. The individual will simply be taxed on what he gets. For example, if an individual is offered either a salary of £20,000 or a salary of £19,000 plus a benefit in kind, then, if he chooses the £20,000 salary he will be taxed on £20,000 and if he chooses the £19,000 salary plus the benefit he will be taxed on £19,000 plus any taxable value of the benefit, whether that taxable value is more or less than £1,000.

In order that an individual is merely taxed on what he gets it may be necessary that a choice to take the benefit is either irrevocable or can be changed only infrequently, that is to say that an individual choosing to take the benefits has no continuing right to exchange them for cash.

These principles can apply equally to a pay rise. If, before an individual is offered a pay rise, he is given the choice of a pay rise or a benefit in kind, he is taxed on what he gets. Thus he will be taxed on the extra pay if he is given the extra pay and on the special value of the benefit if he is given the benefit. This is not the same as being told that he is to receive a pay rise and being asked in what form (cash or kind) he wishes to receive it.

Timing of the contract

In this context, the timing of the contract is crucial. If the individual is offered £20,000 per year, or a pay rise to that amount which may be taken in cash or kind, he will be taxable on the £20,000 regardless of the form in which he takes it. Similarly, if for example an individual has a salary of £1,000 per month and, at the end of the month just before pay day, he asks his employer instead to give him a benefit in kind, he has already earned that £1,000 in salary and he will therefore be taxed on it. The benefit in kind that he then receives may also be taxed and it will be a question of looking at the detailed circumstances to see whether the £1,000 is a contribution to the cost of the benefit which can be deducted from the amount on which the individual is assessed for receiving the benefit. The PAYE position, where the individual takes a benefit in kind in these circumstances is not clear, but the Inland Revenue would contend that PAYE is exigible.

Getting it wrong
An area of risk in these cases is that what was thought to be one thing (perhaps a reduction of salary) was in fact the other (perhaps a contribution). Worst of all, perhaps, the individual is still taxable on the full £20,000 but the £1,000 is not constructed in such a way as to give rise to a deduction from the taxable value of the benefit he receives.

Bonuses and flex
It is sometimes difficult to decide whether salary has already been earned, so that if a benefit is received it must have been paid for out of the salary, or whether it has not been earned. It is particularly difficult where an employer awards discretionary bonuses. If an individual is about to receive a truly discretionary bonus, and, before the bonus is awarded, he is approached by the company and told that it is considering awarding him a bonus either of a specified amount of cash or in the form of a specified benefit, upon which he indicates his preference, he will be taxed on what he gets: on the cash value of the bonus if he receives cash and on the special value of the benefit if he takes the benefit.

If, on the other hand, the payment of the bonus is customary, is nominally discretionary but is in fact always paid if the appropriate targets are met, it will be more difficult to argue that it can at the last minute be sacrificed and replaced by a benefit in kind without being taxed (*Corbett* v *Duff* ((1941) 23 TC 763)). There are many kinds of arrangements, all of which need to be reviewed on their merits: bonus pools, for example, do not fit neatly into either category.

If the individual is awarded a pay rise or bonus of a specified amount and asked whether he wants to receive it in cash or in kind, there might well in the circumstances be an argument that he has in any event got a monetary entitlement and, if he chooses the benefit in kind, has applied it in taking the benefit. He would then be liable to income tax on the gross monetary entitlement which would also be treated for VAT purposes as VAT-inclusive consideration (VATA 1983, s.10).

The exchange value
As a general principle, the value attributed for income tax purposes to any benefit received in kind is the cash for which it can be converted or exchanged (*Tennant* v *Smith* ((1892) 3 TC 158)). This value is the 'exchange value'. The principle that it is the exchange value which is the amount which is taxed is varied in very many circumstances, but it remains important in understanding flexible compensation. The most famous practical example of the application of this principle is that of the employee entitled to acquire a new suit as an emolument (*Wilkins* v *Rogerson* ((1960) 39 TC 344)). The court held that what he could convert into cash was the suit once he got it and, at that point, its resale value was not its price new but a secondhand value. In that case, the secondhand value was an amount equal to about one-third of its price new in the shop. He was therefore taxed on that figure of about one-third of its shop price.

Another example of the principle that the value attributed to a benefit is its exchange value is the right to use an asset. An employee allowed the personal use of an asset which continues to be owned by his employer and which he cannot let out on hire or otherwise turn into cash is, under this general principle, not taxed at all.

Other cases which contain useful comments by judges on the general principles involved are *Weight* v *Salmon* ((1935) 19 TC 174: receipt of shares) *Abbott* v *Philbin* ((1960) 39 TC 82: share options) and *Laidler* v *Perry* ((1965) 42 TC 351: Christmas vouchers).

Benefits exchangeable for salary

A most important development of the principle that benefits in kind are taxable in the amount of the cash for which they can be exchanged is where the individual has and retains the choice of a benefit in kind or additional salary. The leading case here is *Heaton* v *Bell* and the conclusions from that case are set out below. Mr Bell was, under the terms of his company's scheme, able on giving two weeks' notice to give up his car and have his salary paid in full. The case of *Heaton* v *Bell* was heard in the House of Lords. The Law Lords considered the position on the basis that his old, higher, salary had not continued (and had therefore not been applied in part as rent for the car) but had in fact been reduced.

Valuation of benefits

Conclusions about the valuation of benefits that can be fairly clearly drawn from *Heaton* v *Bell* are as follows:

(1) The decision was that the taxable value of the use of the car was that portion of his gross salary which Mr Bell had sacrificed in return for the car but could recover on giving up the car. In other words, the comments made in *Heaton* v *Bell* indicate that benefits in kind are taxable under general principles to the extent of the individual's ability to exchange the benefits for cash remuneration.

(2) A period of notice is likely to be ignored, so that the full amount of replacement salary is taxable, at least if the notice period is short. The longer the notice period, the less clear is the position.

It also follows from *Heaton* v *Bell* that an individual who is able to sacrifice one benefit in kind in exchange for another benefit in kind is not, under general principles, taxable at all unless of course that other benefit is itself convertible into cash.

It further follows from *Heaton* v *Bell* that it is not the sacrificing or giving up of the salary which creates the tax charge. Rather it is the right to receive cash payments instead which causes the benefit to be taxable. The amount which is taxable is the amount which could be received as an alternative to the benefit.

Applying *Heaton* v *Bell*

Heaton v *Bell* has no application to an employee who is offered a choice when his contract is being negotiated, such that once the contract is made, his choice is incorporated in his employment contract such that he has no right to review his choice and does not in fact do so. Such an individual would be taxed on what he receives. In addition, *Heaton* v *Bell* has no application to the tax treatment of individuals who select a cash alternative. They will be taxed on the cash they take, not on the taxable value of any hypothetical benefits which they might have taken.

In practice, few choices, once made, are irrevocably set in stone. Clearly, *Heaton* v

Bell will not apply to tax a benefit by reference to an exchange value if neither employer nor employee has the right or intention to replace the benefit by additional salary. This will remain the case even if, some years later, a change is made; the tax position after that change is made will depend on what the change is and would not be retrospective. In reality, however, there are several situations between the extreme of a perpetual right to change one's mind and an irrevocable choice.

It is clearly quite safe to require that, once, and to the extent that, an individual has chosen to take a benefit or benefits and not salary, he cannot thereafter reverse his decision by increasing the total cash component of his package in return for a reduction of the benefits he receives. Because *Heaton* v *Bell* does not apply to cash remuneration, an individual opting for cash can be allowed to exchange the cash for a benefit in kind without affecting the income tax treatment of his salary or of anyone else's benefits (as long as the arrangements are not tantamount to the application of salary for benefits in kind).

Containing the element of choice

It is likely that the rigour of this rule could be tempered if the choice of reducing the level of benefits and increasing the cash portion of the package were conditionally available on the occurrence of specified events which might, but might not, occur. It may well produce a quite sufficiently flexible policy to give an employee the chance to increase the cash component but only on the occurrence of what might be described as a significant life event which would affect his financial needs. The events could be defined as marriage, the birth of a child, divorce or the death of a parent, wife or child. Other events which could trigger an increase in the cash package might be relocation at the employer's request or promotion if the employer has a defined grading structure where promotion is not automatic.

It may be thought that the absence of a right to exchange a benefit for cash is sufficient to avoid any charge to tax on the cash which could have been taken instead. Nevertheless, *Heaton* v *Bell* indicates that one does not look merely at the legal form of what is happening. The question it asks is whether the employee can convert the benefit into cash or not. If the employer does not normally allow changes to be made, the occasional exception in special circumstances will not prejudice the position. If, on the other hand, any approach to the personnel department to make such a change will normally be accepted, the Commissioners of Inland Revenue, the fact-finding appellate tribunal for income tax, might well decide that the benefit is exchangeable into cash and taxable accordingly.

Further flexibility may be gained if an individual may exercise a choice but only on certain specified dates. For example, if on 2 January an individual can choose either cash or a car but, if he takes the car, is forced to retain the car for 36 months, no one can say on 1 February that he has any right to anything other than what he chose on 2 January.

Similarly, where an employer and employee agree that salary is reduced for, say, the next 12 months and the employer's funding of the pension scheme is increased for the same period, *Heaton* v *Bell* should not apply.

On balance it is considered that a 12-month period as a rule of thumb in determining

Appendix 2: The Tax Treatment of Flexible Compensation

whether *Heaton* v *Bell* principles apply to any given case is a reasonable solution to the problem. This is the view taken by the Inland Revenue.

Special rules for benefits
The rules set out thus far would frequently give rise to unrealistically low values being attributed to benefits in kind. In many cases these rules would cause them not to be taxed at all. The general principles are therefore subject to a whole series of exceptions in particular cases. There are special rules for taxing an individual on the value of accommodation he may use or vouchers or credit tokens which he receives and which can be exchanged for or used to acquire something else (ICTA 1988, s.141–147). There are also complex rules for employee share schemes, pensions and life assurance arrangements, although in each of these cases those rules can be avoided, and the benefit provided tax-free, if the arrangements have been approved by the Inland Revenue in accordance with certain specific statutory provisions (mainly in ICTA 1988, s.135–137, 185–187 and 590–612, but also in several Schedules to ICTA 1988 and in subsequent legislation).

The most important exception to the general principle that benefits in kind are taxed on the cash value for which they may be exchanged applies to the 'higher-paid', an expression which has now disappeared from the Taxes Act but is a useful shorthand to describe any employee earning at the rate of at least £8,500 per year (this figure being inclusive of the taxable value of his benefits calculated on the basis that he is earning at least £8,500 a year) and almost all directors (ICTA 1988, s.167). For the higher-paid, benefits are valued for tax purposes as follows.

(1) Where the individual receives a benefit outright, for example membership of a private health plan or the purchase of an asset which is transferred to him immediately, he is taxed on the related cost to the employer.

(2) Where an individual has the right to use a car in which ownership remains with the employer or a third party, a special charge, known as a 'scale charge' is applied. (See the CCH publication *Car or Cash?: A Guide for Employers and Employees in Making the Choice.*)

(3) For the right to use most other assets when ownership remains with the employer or a third party, an individual is taxed on 20 per cent of the market value of the asset when it is first applied as a benefit, or any rent paid by the person providing it if that rent is greater, plus any expenses connected with the asset's use or maintenance.

(4) Where an asset is transferred to an employee after it has been used or depreciated, he is taxed on the market value of the asset or, unless it is a car, the original value less any 20 per cent or rent charges made under (c) above if that results in a higher figure.

From each of these four figures in (1) to (4) a deduction will frequently, but not always, be made

(1) for any contributions the employee makes for the use of the asset; or

(2) where the benefit is the transfer of an asset, for any payment for the asset made by the employee.

In some cases, a further deduction is available if the asset is used in part for business purposes.

Avoid paying tax on the cash alternative and the special value of the benefit
The question then arises as to what happens if an individual could be charged both on the cash for which the benefit could be converted or exchanged under the rules set out earlier (the 'exchange value') and by reference to the 'special value', namely the value given under either the exceptions referred to above or the alternative rules for the higher-paid. The special value may of course be zero, as is the case with an employer's contributions to an approved pension scheme. In many cases, the special value could be close to the salary which the employer is prepared to offer instead; medical insurance could be a case in point. If there is both an exchange value and a special value, the position is summarised in the following paragraphs.

If the exchange value is higher than or equal to the special value, the employee will be taxed on the exchange value. As noted above, however, there will be no exchange value if the right of choice cannot be exercised more than once per year.

If the exchange value is less than the special value, the position depends on the wording of the charge to tax on the special value. This situation may arise in the case of living accommodation (ICTA 1988, s. 145(1) and 146).

Examples of what is taxed
These principles may be illustrated as follows. Assume that some employees, who are *not* directors, are invited to participate in their employer's private medical insurance scheme which covers them for treatment for ordinary illness (as opposed to illness which results from overseas business travel to which the exemption provided in ICTA 1988, s. 155(6) may apply). Assume further that the share of the company's overall premium paid to the insurance company which is allowable to each individual is agreed to be £400. Assume also that their employer provides no other benefits in kind except a conventional pension scheme provided by the Inland Revenue. Various different possibilities are considered in Examples 1–4 below.

Example 1
Assume that each employee is able to opt out of the medical insurance scheme altogether but will not receive any compensation for so doing.

- An individual on a salary of £5,000 per annum who takes up the benefit will simply be taxed on his £5,000 salary.
- An individual on a salary of £9,000 per annum who takes up the benefit will be taxed on his £9,000 salary and the £400.
- An individual at any salary level who does not take up the benefit will simply be taxed on his basic salary.

Appendix 2: The Tax Treatment of Flexible Compensation

Example 2
Assume now that each employee will be awarded £300 additional salary if he chooses to opt out of the medical insurance scheme, which he may do at any time.

- An individual on a salary of £5,000 per annum who takes up the benefit will be taxed on his £5,000 salary and the £300.
- An individual on a salary of £9,000 per annum who takes up the benefit will be taxed on his £9,000 salary and the £400.
- An individual at any salary level who does not take up the benefit will be taxed on his basic salary plus his additional salary of £300.

Example 3
Assume now that the cash alternative is £500.

- The individual on a salary of £5,000 per annum who takes up the benefit will be taxed on his £5,000 salary and the £500.
- The individual on a salary of £9,000 per annum who takes up the benefit will be taxed on his £9,000 salary and the £500.
- The individual at any salary level who does not take up the benefit will be taxed on his basic salary plus his additional salary of £500.

Example 4
Assume now that each employee who opts out of the medical insurance scheme is entitled not to extra salary but instead to better pension rights (being rights which do not prejudice Inland Revenue approval of the scheme).

- An individual on a salary of £5,000 per annum who takes up the medical insurance benefit will simply be taxed on his £5,000 salary.
- An individual on a salary of £9,000 per annum who takes up the medical insurance benefit will be taxed on his £9,000 and the £400.
- An individual at any salary level who opts for the better pension rights will simply be taxed on his basic salary.

Enhancing benefits

Where an employee chooses to take an enhancement of an existing benefit, for example to take a better car, in lieu of salary, the rules are a little more difficult to apply. Sometimes, the enhancement will really amount to a separate benefit. For example, if an individual who is a member of his employer's private medical scheme can include his spouse and children in the scheme, but, if he does not, or if he subsequently opts out of this part of the benefit, he will receive an additional £200 salary forthwith, the inclusion of the spouse and children will effectively be treated as a separate additional benefit and the principles set out in the examples above will apply separately to the additional benefit or to the cash taken instead.

Value added tax

Any payment or other consideration provided by the employee will generally give rise to VAT at the appropriate rate (standard or zero (VATA 1983, s. 9 and Sch. 5) unless there is a specific exemption (VATA 1983, Sch. 6)). If the employee applies salary or bonus which has already been contracted for or earned in acquiring a benefit, the sum applied in this way will be consideration.

On the other hand, if the employee does not apply salary (or other emoluments) already earned to taking the benefit, but instead receives both a salary and a benefit in kind under his contract of employment, it has hitherto always been accepted that VAT is not in point. There may be input tax on the cost of obtaining the benefits which will normally be deductible in the hands of the employer, or not deductible as the case may be, according to the normal rules. Nevertheless, the employee is not paying consideration, so the provision by the employer to him of a benefit under the terms of a contract of employment which provides that the employee shall receive that benefit (and giving him no choice in the matter) follows the normal VAT rules for the provision of benefits in kind for no consideration.

Co-operative Insurance Society Ltd v *C & E Commrs*

Where flexible compensation is involved, it might be thought that those rules similarly apply. There is, however, an alternative view which Customs had been pressing in many cases up until the decision in *Co-operative Insurance Society Ltd* v *C & E Commrs* ([1992] BVC 694). We understood them to argue that the provision of benefits where an employee has a choice of taking benefits or salary gives rise to VAT on the benefits, even where the employee expresses his wish or makes his choice before his selection takes contractual effect. The grounds for this view appeared to be *either*:

(1) that the salary forgone by an individual taking a benefit is consideration for the supply of the benefit; *or*

(2) that the right to choose between additional salary and the benefits is a chose in action, or right, provided by the employer for a consideration.

It was thought that Customs were arguing (1) and not (2), and this was confirmed by the CIS case.

The consequences of the CIS case

The VAT consequences of the above alternative views would be as follows:

(1) If the salary forgone were consideration provided by the employee to the employer for the benefit, a liability for VAT would arise at the standard rate to the extent that supplies of the benefits taken were chargeable at the standard rate. Therefore, a choice of car or £1,000 cash would give rise to VAT of 17½ ÷ 117½ × £1,000 to the extent that employees took cars, while the provision of life assurance is exempt and the payment of cash and the provision of extra days of holiday are, probably, outside the scope of VAT altogether.

(2) If the employer's granting the right of choice were the taxable provision of a right, VAT would be chargeable at the standard rate, currently 17½ ÷ 117½, on the entire additional salary whether it was taken in cash or in kind.

Which rules apply must depend on the contractual position. If the employee is given a choice of a benefit in kind or additional salary as part of the negotiation of his

Appendix 2: The Tax Treatment of Flexible Compensation

remuneration package or of his pay rise, but, once he has made his choice, that selection is reflected in his contract, no VAT can arise from his being given the choice. It cannot be right to say that remuneration which an employee is not entitled to and does not receive is consideration which he provides. He cannot give what he never had and was never entitled to receive for the benefits which he does take.

This analysis has been confirmed by the case of *Co-operative Insurance Society Ltd* v *C & E Commrs*. The possibility of an appeal against that decision was effectively quashed by the making very shortly afterwards of the Value Added Tax (Treatment of Transactions) Order 1992 (SI 1992/630). This provides that where an employer gives an employee a choice between (1) a salary and (2) a lower salary plus the right to the private use of a car provided by the employer, and the employee chooses (2), the provision of the right to use the car privately is not a supply for VAT purposes, provided that the consideration for the provision of the car is only the difference in salary in choices (1) and (2).

Customs' reaction to these developments was that:

(1) they accept that the provisions of SI 1992/630 apply to the intermediate situation of employees choosing a smaller car and sacrificing less salary;

(2) sacrificing 'routine' employee benefits other than salary for a car will not be regarded as consideration;

(3) they will not pursue the VAT allegedly due in other appeals outstanding at the date of the CIS decision; but

(4) where a company makes a direct charge for the use of a car, whether by deduction from salary or otherwise, VAT will still have to be accounted for.

While the decision in the case and the subsequent statutory instrument and Customs' communications have clarified the VAT position, at least as far as cars are concerned, the following cautionary points should be noted:

(1) Customs maintain that the CIS case can be distinguished on its particular facts; therefore in other circumstances where the facts were different they might try to take the case to a VAT tribunal;

(2) subject to what has been said above about Customs' interpretation of SI 1992/630, the order applies only to the straightforward case of a simple choice between cash and car and has no application to other benefits or to instances in which the consideration is in a form other than salary sacrifice.

Care is, therefore, still needed. If in truth the individual has applied remuneration in obtaining the benefit, then clearly VAT will in principle be exigible.

In any event, the preceding paragraphs on VAT have merely set out some general principles. It should be clear that, as with any other taxation matter, the particular circumstances of each case must be reviewed before the VAT position can be settled.

National Insurance contributions

National Insurance contributions ('NIC') will be due in the normal way on payments to those who take salary rather than benefits in kind.

The principles which determine, for income tax purposes, whether salary has been earned and applied in contributing to the cost of a benefit or has never been earned in the first place, apply equally for NIC. The major difference, however, is that NIC are not exigible on benefits in kind (The Social Security (Contributions) Regulations 1979 (SI 1979/591), reg. 19(1)(d)) (subject to certain exceptions relating to securities and life and annuity business within SI 1979/591, reg. 19(5) and Sch. 1A and to the exception, from 6 April 1991, relating to company cars). The DSS may, however, have a case to seek NIC if the payment of cash can be demanded immediately and free of risk.

An NIC trap arises in the valuation of benefits.

Employers offering a choice of cash or benefits may set the amount of cash available by reference to the cost to them of providing the benefit. Logically, it would follow that the cash payable in lieu of the benefit should be discounted to reflect the employer's NIC which will arise where cash is paid.

A simple deduction of employer's NIC is, however, illegal (Social Security Contributions and Benefits Act 1992, Sch. 1, para. 3(2)). There is a difference between providing a choice of a benefit costing £100 and a cash payment of £100 less employer's NIC (illegal) and a choice of that same benefit and a cash payment of £90.58.

Flexible compensation and notional salaries

One particular method of implementing a flexible compensation system is the use of notional salaries. This system is worth discussing as it illustrates a number of the points relating to income tax, NIC and VAT which have been dealt with in this appendix.

The use of notional salaries is also a method of dealing with the requirements of individuals who wish to take benefits to a greater value than that allowed under their employer's arrangements. In the absence of a notional salary arrangement, the company could charge the employee for the excess. The results of this would be, following the cases of *Cordy* v *Gordon* and *Machon* v *McLoughlin*:

(1) income tax and NIC would be payable on the full basic salary;
(2) the income tax deduction from the special value of the benefit might not be available if the contribution did not satisfy the relevant statutory tests;
(3) the employer would be liable to account for VAT on the charge.

Under a notional salary arrangement, employees would typically have a basic salary, a core of benefits applicable to all employees, and in addition an allowance of a given value, probably expressed in monetary terms. This allowance could be taken in the form of a mixture of cash and benefits chosen from the flex package.

It is necessary, in order to adopt the notional salary arrangement, to change the contractual arrangements between the employer and employee. All employees would get a notional salary which would be used for the following purposes:

(1) comparability;
(2) salary reviews;
(3) calculating pension contributions and other salary-related benefits (such as death benefits, personal accident insurance, or share options);
(4) where applicable, calculating an overtime rate.

It would not, however, constitute contractual pay: it would not be an amount which the employee was entitled to receive as salary.

Notional salaries are often used in organisations at present, particularly for calculating pension and life cover and for staff who are long-term sick, seconded overseas or on maternity leave. Their use is therefore not an artificial device.

As well as this notional salary, employees would have an actual salary. In the case of employees who do not overshoot their benefit allowance, actual salary would be equal to notional salary, while the actual salary of those employees who do would be their notional salary less the value of their overshoot. The actual salary would be the amount of salary which the employer was contracted to pay. It would be shown as such on salary advice letters (although such letters could also note the notional salary) and would appear on the payslip. Until and unless it was changed (for example, when a pay rise was awarded) it would be the only salary to which the employee would be entitled.

By adopting this approach, and by not allowing employees to change this arrangement other than by entering into a new contract, for example at annual review, it is considered that the problems arising from *Heaton* v *Bell* are avoided. Great care will be needed in all the formal and informal documentation to ensure that the contractual salary is precisely that and that the notional salary is no more than a base used for the purposes outlined.

The legal relationship

There is also the question of how to make the salary sacrifice or bonus sacrifice legally binding. Employment agreements are contracts, so a new remuneration package will need the agreement of both parties. It must make sense to document this in a form which both parties sign. Discretionary bonuses are, however, outside the existing contract (although it may record the possibility of their being paid) and, if an employee indicates how he wishes to receive the bonus before he becomes entitled to it, there is no legal agreement to document.

Appendix 3: Flexible Benefits Administration Systems

There are now a number of systems available in the UK to administer flexible benefits plans. This appendix sets out brief details of some of those systems. The list is not exhaustive, and your information technology experts and professional advisers may be able to suggest alternatives and to comment on the suitability of proprietary systems for your company's needs.

1. Coopers & Lybrand – FLEXPORT

Company details
Coopers & Lybrand
Plumtree Court
London
EC4A 4HT

Tel: 071 583 5000
Fax: 071 212 4418

Contact name
Moira Conoley — Partner, Reward Practice
Carol L Woodley — Principal, Actuarial and Benefits Consultancy Division

System name
Flexport

Functions

Enrolment:
- Personalised selection forms
- Employee access for 'what ifs'
- Verification against entitlements
- Confirmation statement
- Calculation module

Also available:
- 'Benefits information line' for telephone access and information for employees

Database maintenance:
- Personnel data import
- Option price update
- Input of confirmed selections

Appendix 3: Flexible Benefits Administration Systems 133

Reporting: Payroll
                               Financial
                               Take up
                               Insurer

Plan maintenance: Additional options
                               Additional benefits
                               Altering credit formula

Outputs
Customised: Selection forms
                               Confirmation statements
                               Reports
                               Employee communications materials

Technical specification
This system may be run on an IBM compatible PC using DOS 3.0 or higher, and, for multi-user applications, through local area networks. For full specification, contact Coopers & Lybrand.

2. Hewitt Associates – CORE FLEX

Company details
Hewitt Associates
Romeland House
Romeland Hill
St Albans
AL3 4EZ

Tel: (0727) 866233
Fax: (0727) 830122

Contact name
Phil Murray   Flexible Compensation Practice Leader
Tim Halliday   Head of Information Systems

Functions
Definition of payroll cycles and 'working' calendar
Control of eligibility to join the scheme
Definition of award[1] calculation algorithms
Control of option[2] eligibility
Fixed or personalised option prices
Manual entry or import of personnel data
Calculation, import and entry of awards

134   Flexible Benefits

Automatic pro-rating of awards for joiners and leavers
Authorisation and maintenance of award amounts
Determination of eligible options for each employee
Printing of employee preference[3] forms
Entry and import of employee preferences
Analysis of preferred options
Authorisation and maintenance of preferences
Production of authorised 'award' statements
Award allocation
Reversal of allocations
Reporting/export of allocations
Editing of preference form and award statements

Outputs
Scheme eligibility report
Employee details audit report
Employee scheme status
Employee register
Award authorisation report
Award reconciliation report (new and completed awards)
Employee preference forms
Preference (option) analysis
Preference authorisation
Award statements (confirming authorised choices)
Allocations
Account statement ('Bank style' credits and debits)
Account balance exception report
Account transaction summary
Scheme configuration
Ad-hoc reports can be produced using Query/400 IBM's AS/400 reporting tool)

Notes:
1. Awards   The value of the flexible compensation element of the employee's package (expressed in money or points terms).
2. Options   The menu of choices available to employees in the scheme. Each option has an associated price.
3. Preferences The employee's preferred mix of options, with a total price equal to the award.

Special features
CoreFlex is a package which has been designed and developed primarily for the UK

market by Hewitt Associates. Capable of administering the simplest to the most complex of schemes, CoreFlex is itself flexible, allowing a high degree of customisation on installation and as the scheme evolves.

Customer Preference Forms and Award Statements can be produced by exporting the appropriate data and merging it using a word processor or desk top publishing package.

The system facilitates the 'management discretion' approach to avoiding problems associated with income tax, NIC and VAT.

CoreFlex Accounts are used for options, such as private petrol, where a regular allocation is made to the employee, but claims (expenses in the case of private petrol) are made irregularly.

Facilities are provided to assist the personnel function in tracking and extracting P11D data.

Automatic deferral of awards without authorised preferences.

Comprehensive audit trails.

Employees can be 'batched' together and processed en masse.

Technical specifications
Runs on IBM AS/400 computers
Scheme size is limited only by the disk capacity of AS/400
Multi-user, relational database
Uses commitment control to ensure complete database integrity
Written using market-leading CASE tool, allowing platform-independence
Future availability of OS/2 and UNIX versions
Mutilingual

CoreFlex can be licensed for use by the client in-house or can be provided as a third party administration service. The price is dependent on the number of employees being administered within the scheme. Client support and ongoing development of the system will be funded by an annual maintenance fee.

3. Noble Lowndes – Flexible Remuneration System

Company details
Noble Lowndes & Partners Limited
PO Box 144
Norfolk House
Wellesley Road
Croydon
CR9 3EB

Tel: 081 686 2466
Fax: 081 681 1458

Contact name
Andy Christie
Ron MacDonald

Functions
Maintains comprehensive employee records:
> Manual entry or automated import of data
> Basic employee data
> Dependant data
> Beneficiary data.

Calculates the value of the flexible remuneration for an employee on one or more different bases as required:
> Per capita amount
> Percentage of pay based on age, service or any other data element
> Flat amounts based on age, service or any other data element
> Amounts based on elections made by employee
> Other customer-defined amounts.

Can deal with any number of benefit options:
> Individually defined eligibility, pricing, restrictions and levels of benefit
> Options can be linked together to form any number of 'plans'.

Employee participation and benefit selection:
> Manual entry or automated import of data
> Histories of benefit selections maintained
> Selection/confirmation of benefit forms
> Identification of status changes.

Processing of spending accounts such as private petrol:
> Manual entry or automated import of data
> Claims validations to eliminate duplicate claims
> Tracking payments made against entitlements
> Cheque printing, cheque audit trail, export to in-house expenses system.

Various reports and premium statements:
> Benefit provider premium reports
> Eligibility listings
> Additions/deletions
> Cost centre/department billings or reports
> P11D
> Ad-hoc reports.

Special features
This PC-based Flexible Benefits Remuneration System is a powerful system that can accommodate any type of plan, and can be used to provide administration for non-flex plans as well.

The system can interface with human resources/payroll systems and can operate independently or networked to a specific location or department while ensuring complete confidentiality.

In addition to the standard reports, users can export data and merge with in-house systems, or standard word processing and desk top publishing packages.

Technical specification
The system is PC based and a full specification is available from Noble Lowndes on request.

4. Towers Perrin – TOP FLEX

Company details
Towers Perrin
Castlewood House
77–91 New Oxford Street
London WC1A 1PX

Tel: 071 379 4000/4411
Fax: 071 379 7478/0532

Contact name
Paul McCourt

Functions
Import of employee data from other office systems
Confirmation of benefit eligibility
Production of personalised enrolment forms
 – specific to benefit eligibility
 – allowing for fixed or personalised pricing structures
Manual entry or import of employee selections
Verification of selections against entitlements
Production of personalised confirmation statements.

Outputs
Analysis of employee selections
Outputs required to payroll and other personnel functions
Management information regarding cost implications of selections
Outputs to benefit providers regarding selections, e.g. insurance company for life cover
Other reports as requested.

138   *Flexible Benefits*

Special features
Where possible, the system aims to integrate with existing office administration systems.

The system is customised to meet individual company requirements regarding:

>benefits on offer;
>enrolment and confirmation statements;
>reporting requirements; and
>systems capabilities.

5.   William M. Mercer Limited – FLEXKEY™ For Windows™

Company details
William M. Mercer Limited
Riverside Court
Guildford Road
Leatherhead
Surrey
KT22 9DF

Tel: (0372) 379044
Fax: (0372) 379125

Contact name
Ginny Olds

Functions

Current year enrolment:	Perform calculations
Annual enrolment:	Personalised forms
	Election entry and editing
	Confirmation statements
	Default processing
Data maintenance:	Data import
	Employee reconciliation
	On-line maintenance
Reporting:	Payroll
	Management
	Insurance company
	Enrolment
	Ad-hoc
Plan maintenance:	Plan year end
	New plan year initialisation
	Parameter
	Security administration

On line help

Outputs are customised to company requirements, and include:

Enrolment forms
Confirmation statements
Reports

Special features
Used on a personal computer
Several levels of user interaction
Administers simple or complex programs
Modules easily added
Customised to meet specific needs
Security protected
Extensive on line help
Interfaces customised based on file and transaction format
Personalised printing

Technical specifications
Supplied upon request from potential user.

6. The Wyatt Company – WYFLEX

Company details
The Wyatt Company
21 Tothill Street
Westminster
London
SW1H 9LL

Tel: 071 222 8033
Fax: 071 222 9182

Contact name
David Bright
Don McClune

Functions
Administration system to handle flexible benefit programmes
Database of total compensation information
Calculates benefits values and costs

Outputs
Personalised statements to employees confirming flexible benefit choices
Total compensation statements covering all cash and non-cash benefits
Reports for line managers
Other management reports to plan and monitor costs, etc.
Reports for personnel departments and auditors

Flexible Benefits

P11D information
Reports as required to insurance companies and other benefit providers
Distribution list for each report.

Reports can be:
    viewed on PC terminal;
    printed out directly as hard copy;
    downloaded for use with specialist printing system.

Special features

Tailored reports to meet the requirements of each organisation.

Easy-to-use screens allow employees to test and make own flexible benefit choices, including comparison of gross and net pay positions.

Consolidates and checks accuracy of data from other sources.

Option to add WyCar system which helps employees to make choice between a company car and cash alternative.

Back-up by experienced consultants on scheme design, legal and tax requirements and employee communications.

Technical specifications

Works on IBM PC or compatible personal computers
Can be installed on single PC or networked
Runs under Microsoft Windows 3.1.

The system is fully supported by:
    a user's manual describing the operation procedures in plain English;
    a helpline to call to answer operational questions.

Index

References are to paragraph numbers.

A

Paragraph

Accommodation
. tax efficient benefit .... .221
. tax free benefit .... .220

Administration system
. case study......................... .1408
. choice of solution, options .... .1403
. generally .... 230; 1401; App. 3
. nature of.......................... .1402
. preparation and procedures .... .1406
. selection
. . key functions..................... .1404
. . linking in .... .1405
. third-party...................... .1407

Approach to flexible benefits .... .101

B

Bonus
. benefit received in lieu of, income tax......................... 1102(1)

Business assets
. personal use, tax efficient benefit ...... .221

C

Canteens
. tax-free benefit .... .220

Car parking
. generally .... 708(6)
. tax-free benefit .... .220

Cars – see **Company cars**

Case studies
. administration...................... .1408
. choice of benefit .... .311
. communication .... .1517
. implementation of plan 1601–1613
. objectives......................... .406

Paragraph

Cash
. as an alternative 205; 306
. . income tax..................... 1102(3)
. . National Insurance contributions..... 1104

Child care vouchers
. generally .... 708(2)
. pricing .... .811
. tax-free benefit .... .220

Choice of benefit
. attitude in the UK, survey .... .308
. benefit .... .310
. case study......................... .311
. clean cash......................... .306
. company cars, restriction........... 702(3)
. core benefits .... .306
. core plus benefits .... .306
. employees wanting greater choice ..... .304
. employers offering greater choice...... .303
. free choice .... .306
. generally .... .301
. meaning of choice .... .302
. modular benefits .... .306
. opposition to scheme use, reasons ..... .309
. payment, choice .... .307
. plan design........................ .604
. scope .... .305

Clean cash benefit – see **Cash**

Communication
. administration, planning .... .1511
. case study........................ .1517
. consulting with employees at every stage of project .... .1509
. external context .... .1501
. key messages .... .1513
. media matched to message .... .1514
. monitoring scheme .... .1516
. opinions
. . employees', researching .... .1506
. . sounding out.................... .1504
. partners, inclusion in decision-making process .... .1515

Communication – continued   **Paragraph**
. phased process 1512
. piloting media 1510
. project 1502
. . decision, informing employees.......1508
. project team, establishing 1503
. senior executive sponsorship..........1505
. two-way process 1507

Company cars
. car or cash .... 702(4); App. 1
. choice restriction..................702(3)
. inclusion in plans..................702(1)
. parking.....................220; 708(6)
. pricing
. . leasing ....808(1)
. . purchasing......................808(2)
. structuring options ....702(2)
. tax efficient benefit 221

Contract of employment
. changes 229; 1201
. . employment law – see
    Employment law

Core benefits 204; 306

Core plus benefits 306

Cost control
. generally 213
. international assignment policy 1301

Costing benefits package
. current
. . analysing data......................504
. . establishing a baseline 501
. . inclusions 503
. . understanding current cost 502
. new
. . closing the loop...................1005
. . developing a cost model 1002
. . generally 214; 1001
. . testing for robustness...............1004
. . winners and losers 1003

Crèche facilities – see **Child care vouchers**

Credit allowances
. currency...........................607
. methods used to derive credit
    allocations
. . formula approach..................906
. . tabular approach 907
. setting
. . generally 901
. . meaning of credits 902
. . methods used to derive credit
    allocations 905–907

                  Paragraph
. . procedure 903
. . winners and losers concept 904

Credit card subscriptions
. tax-free benefit 220

D

Definitions and meanings
. choice.............................302
. credits............................902
. flexible benefits.....................203

Dental insurance .... 708(4)

Designing the plan
. key parameters
. . benefits included 605
. . design parameters 602
. . eligibility 603
. . examples.........................608
. . importance of revisiting objectives 601
. . pricing credits.....................607
. . scope for choice 604
. . timing of elections 606
. major benefits
. . car parking .... 708(6)
. . child care......................708(2)
. . company cars 702
. . dental insurance.................708(4)
. . education assistance..............708(3)
. . fitness facilities ....708(5)
. . generally 701
. . holiday entitlement 707
. . life assurance 704
. . long-term disability insurance 706
. . medical insurance..................705
. . optical insurance ....708(4)
. . pensions 703
. . professional advice for employees .. 708(1)

Disability insurance
. inclusion in plan .... 0706(1)
. issues for consideration .... 706(3)
. structuring options .... 706(2)

Discrimination........................1205

E

Education assistance.................. 708(3)

Employment law
. contract of employment changes........1201
. . employees' consent 1202
. . establishing......................1205
. . incorporating new terms 1205

Index

	Paragraph
. . recording of terms introduced by plan	1205
. . terms, establishing	1205
. discrimination	1205
. drafting plan	1206
. employees' refusal to accept package	1203
. employees' signature, need to obtain	1205
. equal pay	1204
. introduction of plan	
. . form	1205
. . risks	1207
. . timing	1205
. sex discrimination	1204
Equal pay	1204
Europe	
. application of plans throughout	211

F

Final salary pensions	703(2)
Financial advice	
. pricing	811
First-aid allowances	
. tax-free benefit	220
Fitness facilities – see **Sports facilities**	
Focus groups	1507
Free choice benefits	306

H

Health insurance – see **Medical insurance**

Holiday entitlement	
. inclusion in plan	707
. pricing	810
. tax-free benefit	220

Husband and Wife – see **Spouses**

I

Importing plans	210
Incentives	
. pensions	703(3)
Income tax	
. benefit received in lieu of bonus	1102(1)
. cash taken as an alternative	1102(3)
. flexible compensation	App. 2
. generally	1101; 1102
. part of salary sacrificed	1102(2)

	Paragraph
Inland Revenue	
. limits on pension benefits	703(5)
Insurance	
. dental/optical	708(4)
. disability – see Disability insurance	
. life – see Life assurance	
. medical – see Medical insurance	
Interest – see **Loan interest**	
International assignment policy	
. cost control	1301
. introduction of plan	1304
. motivation	1302
International managers	
. overseas assignments – see International assignment policy	
Introduction of plan	
. employment law – see Employment law	
. generally	102; 105
. key issues – see Key issues	
. major phases in project	104

K

Key issues	
. administration	230
. application of plans throughout Europe	211
. benefits included in package	216
. benefits to avoid	217
. cash benefits	205
. considering benefits	207
. core benefits	204
. costs	214
. cost savings	213
. employees understanding benefits arrangements	225
. existing contracts of employment, changing	229
. flexible benefits, meaning	203
. generally	201
. importing plans from the US	210
. inhibiting factors	224; 228
. introduction of plan	
. . compulsory	226
. . timing	215
. . unionised company	227
. organisations with plans	209
. pensions, inclusion	219
. pitfalls	231
. pricing benefits	223
. professional advice	232

Flexible Benefits

Key issues – continued   Paragraph
. size of organisation and sector,
     suitability........................212
. steps to take following introduction
     of one or two benefits..............218
. tax benefits, moves to neutralise........206
. tax efficient benefits..................221
.. introduction of plan affecting.........222
. tax-free benefits.....................220
. workforce interest....................208

L

Leased cars
. pricing..........................808(1)

Legislative requirements – see **Employment law**

Life assurance
. inclusion in plan..................704(1)
. issues for consideration............704(2)
. tax-free benefit.....................220

Loan interest
. tax efficient benefit..................221
. tax-free benefit.....................220

Long service gifts
. tax-free benefit.....................220

Long-term disability insurance – see **Disability insurance**

Luncheon vouchers
. tax-free benefit.....................220

M

Meals
. tax-free benefit.....................220

Meanings – see **Definitions and meanings**

Medical examinations
. tax-free benefit.....................220

Medical insurance
. inclusion in plan..................705(1)
. issues for consideration............705(3)
. structuring options................705(2)
. tax-free benefit.....................220

Membership fees
. tax-free benefit.....................220

Modular benefits......................306

Money purchase pensions............703(1)

Motives..............................401

              Paragraph
N

National Insurance contributions
. flexible compensation..............App. 2
. generally....................1101; 1104

Nurseries – see **Child care vouchers**

O

Objectives
. case study..........................406
. examples...........................403
. incentives..........................401
. need for............................404
. reconsidering.......................405
. revisiting..........................406
.. plan design........................601
. stated..............................402

Optical insurance..................708(4)

Outplacement counselling
. tax-free benefit.....................220

Overseas assignments
. international managers – see
     International assignment policy

P

Partners – see **Spouses**

Paying for benefits
. choice..............................307

Pensions
. contributions, tax-free benefit.........220
. ethical issues.....................703(4)
. final salary pensions..............703(2)
. inclusion in plan....................219
. Inland Revenue limits.............703(5)
. money purchase pensions..........703(1)
. scheme as an incentive............703(3)

Personal use of business assets
. tax efficient benefit..................221

Pricing benefits – see **Pricing system**

Pricing credits – see **Credit allowances**

Pricing system
. child care vouchers..................811
. company cars
.. leased.........................808(1)
.. purchasing.....................808(2)
. currency............................607
. effects of selection..................807
. financial advice.....................811

Index   145

	Paragraph
. generally	.223
. holiday entitlement	.810
. philosophy	
. . overview	.802
. . pragmatic approach	.805
. . resolving conflicts between principles	.804
. principles	.803
. setting prices	.806
. sports clubs	.811
. unknown quantity	.801
Private education	708(3)
Professional advice	
. as a benefit	708(1)
. seeking	.232
. tax-free benefit	.220
Project team	
. communication	.1503
. generally	103; 104
Purchasing company cars	
. pricing	808(2)

R

Redundancy	
. outplacement counselling	.220
Refreshments	
. tax-free benefit	.220
Risk benefits	
. pricing – see Pricing system	

S

Salary sacrifice	
. partial, income tax	1102(2)
School fees	708(3)
Senior executives	
. opinions	.1504
. sponsorship	.1505

	Paragraph
Sex discrimination	.1204
Sports clubs/facilities	
. generally	708(5)
. pricing	.811
. tax-free benefit	.220
Spouses	
. included in decision-making process	.1515
. travel, tax-free benefit	.220
Staff entertainment	
. tax-free benefit	.220

T

Tax efficient benefits	
. affected by introduction of plan	.222
. generally	.221
Tax-free benefits	
. generally	.220
Terms and conditions of employment – see Contract of employment	

U

Uniforms	
. tax-free benefit	.220
Unionised companies	
. introduction of plan	.227

V

Value added tax	
. flexible compensation	App. 2
. generally	1101; 1103

W

Winners and losers concept	
. costing scheme	.1003
. setting credit allowances	.904
Workforce interest	.208